Shot & Grape Tour

Bordeaux to Burley-in-Wharfedale

Copyright © 2006 Tangent Books
All rights reserved

Publishers: Steve Faragher, Richard Jones

Design/maps: Joe Burt

Production/editing: Anne Smith

Produced by: Faragher Jones Ltd
Tel: 01225 319799

ISBN 0-9553520-2-9

The first moral right of the author has been asserted

First published in Great Britain in 2006 by
Tangent Books 3 Monmouth Place, Bath BA1 2AT
www.tangentbooks.co.uk

Printed by Gutenberg Press Limited

This book is dedicated to all the brave men that gave their lives in the many battlefields I crossed during this wonderful tour. And to my wife Lizzie and our children Tom and Evie, even though they DID send me away again.

Introduction

After retiring early in late 2003 I was sent on what, for me, was a monumental cycle journey from Lands End to John O'Groats. You may ask yourself why I was 'sent' on such a journey. Well, indeed I am using some literary licence here in that my wife and young family were just not used to me being around, all day and every day. So I said I would get out from under their feet and ride my bike from Lands End to John O'Groats. At the time it seemed a good idea until, of course, I started working out the detail of how to do it! But, I did 'do it' and, while passing my spare time in various B&Bs and inns along the way, I kept a daily diary of my journey. On my return, the diary became my first book, published under the title *End to End* (ISBN: 0-9544177-8-X) in late 2004.

After the dust settled and 2004 became 2005, I was restless to travel again. This time I was packed off to tramp around the battlefields of South Africa with my favourite Zulu War Author, Ian Knight together with my son Tom and his grandfather and my father-in-law, Mike.

Filled with dreams of further adventure (and of fine wine and food!), I decided to undertake another cycling trip in 2006. This time, I wanted to combine my interests in cycling, with my appetite for fine wines and food, and my other great interest, history. So I started to plan in early 2006 a 'Battlefields and Vineyards' tour in, where else but, France. Starting in St Quentin de Baron near Bordeaux and ending up in Burley-in-Wharfedale near Ilkley in Yorkshire. Why these two particular places you may ask. Well, I am very fortunate to have homes in both of these small towns and it seemed the natural thing to do. The rest, as they say, is history, as this record of my next 17 days will attest.

I do have a number of thank yous to record, not least of which goes to the hoteliers, innkeepers and restaurateurs whose services eased my aching limbs and renewed my energy on a daily basis. Particular thanks must go the mechanics in the Renault and Peugeot garages in Moulin and Le Cateau who were extremely helpful in letting me use their facilities following those dreaded punctures. And to the delightful receptionist at the Croix de Blanche hotel in Fontevraud who single-handedly tackled the gruesome task of washing my cycling kit.

Thanks to my T-Mobile MDA, without whose technology I could not have written this book and without which I could not have kept in touch with civilization. Plus its Sat Nav capabilities kept me on the straight and narrow particularly in large towns and cities (Poitiers springs to mind in particular).

And finally a special note of thanks to P&O Ferries for bringing me back safe and sound to Blighty. Oh, what joy to set foot again on English (make that Yorkshire) soil. Damp and wet, but my soil!

Contents

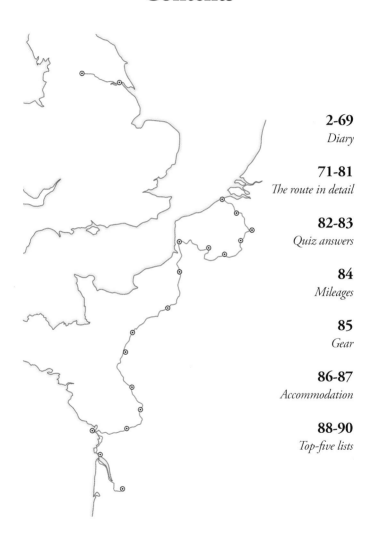

_Day 1

Date: 15 May 2006

95 miles

Left Le Prieure at 8.20am. Graham and Jules waved me off. Jules thought I looked rather fetching in my yellow cycling gear. Not sure what Graham thought but he did want to take pictures!

I was only on the road five minutes and I see my first grumpy Frenchman. Not my fault I nearly hit him as he was in the middle of the road. He had a little goatee beard and then it hit me... it was the Cornish beatnik barman who tailed me two years ago, except he has had his pony tailed surgically moved to his chin! Better get a move on.

A lovely sunny day so stop for coffee by the river in Bordeaux to admire the view... lots of lovely ladies skate by. An uneventful morning, I forget how quiet French roads are.

Wind changes direction as I approach the Atlantic to a north westerly, drat. I feel twinge in hamstring, double drat. I stop for a banana while I contemplate life, or the lack of it in my right hamstring. Only another 40 miles to go! Then out of the blue, I meet my first comrade in arms. A fellow traveller of the road pulls up to offer assistance. Any good with hamstrings or north westerlies?, I say in my best French... which sounds like broad Yorkshire actually. Turns out he is a French Canadian and he started his bike ride in December! Heading for Toulouse, he says, although I mention that Quebec is the other way.

Four hours later, I reach Verdon at the tip of the Gironde estuary but miss the 6.25pm ferry to Royan. Not surprising as I've covered 95 miles – a record for this Webster. Have to wait for the 8pm ferry so decide to whistle while I wait. From *Snow White*, in case you were wondering and, before you all bombard me with emails, yes, I know it's whistle while you work. But, in case you forgot, I've retired.

Finally, I reach the hotel with a beach view and blue and white curtains at 8.20pm. Quick bath and down to the casino. Yes, Royan does have one, for 9.30pm.

Feeling weary now so must sign off but, before I go, I am starting this trip off with a quiz. BBFN and watch the news.

Quiz: Let me know your favourite film with a casino scene.

Off the Road

Lunch: The Pavillon de Margaux – aah! Margaux, one of my favourite places in all the world. Famous, of course for its beautiful wines of which Chateau Margaux is the crème de la crème. Dreaming for a 1982 Chateau Margaux, I settle instead for a Pavillon de Margaux Blanc. After all I have got black lycra cycling shorts on and it really just is not done to quaff Margaux sans formal dress. I am shown rather quizzically to a table in the Conservatory where I order the "Plats de Jour". Which turns out to be Dorade with peas and other summer vegetables. Very nice indeed. Following crème Brulee and a noisette (like the Italian Macchiatto) I am suitably refreshed to travel on.

Dinner: Opposite the Casino at Pontaillac. Feeling ever so slightly knackered I grab a quick Duck Confit and Frites at the nearest restaurant I can find off the Esplanade at Pontaillac. Washed down with a House Red I am soon drifting into slumber so almost sleep walking I head back to my hotel. Within seconds I am asleep, dreaming of Margaux, the wine, not the actress!

Ferry Boat over the Gironde Estuary between Le Verdon and Royan

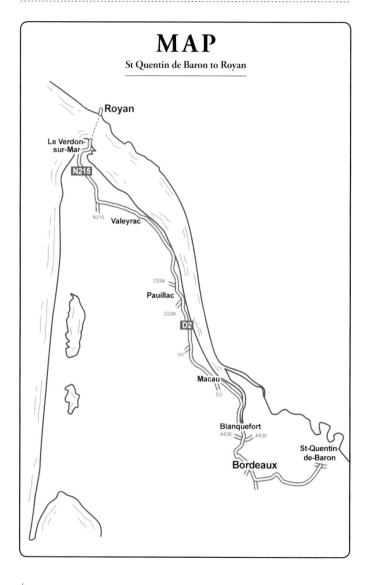

MAP

St Quentin de Baron to Royan

Royan

Le Verdon-
sur-Mar

N215

N215 Valeyrac

D204

Pauillac

D206

D2

D5

Macau

D2

Blanquefort
A630   A630

Bordeaux

St-Quentin-
de-Baron

_Day 2

Royan to Isle de Re

Date: 16 May 2006

78 miles

Left Royan at 9am after a hearty breakfast of bread and jam. Are not the French great at breakfasts... not? Cycled two miles to seaside resort of St Palais. Stopped for coffee. Could murder a bacon sandwich but settle for pain au chocolate.

Pleasant ride through forest to the zoo at Palmyre. Saw giraffes and pink flamingos before a zoo worker spotted me and asked for the admission fee. Pretended I did not understand him, which was easy enough, and did a runner.

Next up, elevenses in La Tremblade. On the edge of the famous Le Parc aux Huîtres. For the uninitiated, 75sq miles of oyster heaven. Then it started to rain. And did it rain! It turned very dark and thunder and lightning accompanied the ever-increasing downpour. Crossed over the oyster lagoon fearing I may get struck by lightning. Reached Marenne drenched. Think about stopping but decide to press on to Rochfort for some lunch.

Pass through quaint fortified villages, fortified against Les Rosbifs, I might add. So, after asking a coach driver how to get out of one particular town instead of how to break in, I say I'm Scottish, just in case. Press on to La Rochelle for a pint. In dire need after coping with the afternoon sun. Would you believe it, after this morning's downpour. Hope my copy of *Blue-and-white-Wizards* didn't get damp in my saddle bag. You can always find a verse or two in there to cheer you up. Better than the Bible. Very civilised spot looking out over the harbour and the lovely ladies passing by.

Last 13 miles over the Pont to the Isle de Re. A quite idyllic island giving priority to bikes instead of cars. I'm all for that! Arrive very tired at 7pm in Saint-Martin de Ré. Covered 78 miles today at an average speed of 11.2mph. Hotel is very designerish but, after a long soak, I feel refreshed enough to venture out so I take a harbour view table in La Baleine Bleue. More tomorrow. Hope I find a bar to watch the Champions League final!

Quiz: After yesterday's pathetic response to the casino survey tonight, I am setting you a follow-on question. Who made his screen entrance in a casino scene and went on to become the biggest draw on the screen in the 1960s? Easy you say, but what was the of the lady asking who he was? Put that into your internet search engine and smoke it!

Off the Road

Lunch: Main Square in Rochefort. Find outdoor restaurant/café in the main square in Rochefort. Basic fare in the Café is quite good though and the sun peeps through to allow me to dry off. Cheese omelette and frites with a cheap Cote de Bourg. I need fortifying after my experience in the thunder and lightning this morning.

Dinner: The Baleine Bleue in St Martin de Re. My first Oysters of the trip, Marennes, of course, from just down the road. I wonder if they got rained on today too! And then Lobster, what else here by the sea in designer belt Isle de Re. Simply grilled with some sauteed potatoes and washed down with a quality white Riesling from the Alsace region of France, a Trimbach. Sheer luxury, and do I need it after today's ride. A wonderful meal in a very scenic harbour. I must make the most of it because after tonight I won't be seeing the sea again for almost two weeks.

The gorgeous little harbour at Saint-Martin de Re

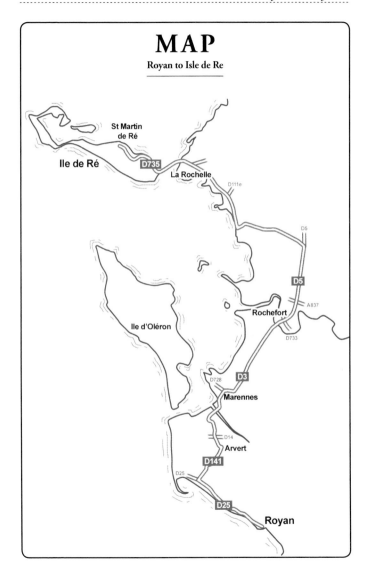

MAP

Royan to Isle de Re

_Day 3

Date: 17 May 2006

73 miles

Left idyll of Saint-Martin de Ré at 8.30am. Breakfast spoilt by surly waitress and delay in getting caffeine fix. Stopped at Rivedoux for more caffeine before I tackle the Pont Viaduc over to the mainland with a strong easterly blowing. That's three days running that the wind has been against me. Make a mental note to undertake more climatological research before next velo adventure.

Decide to stop in Dompierre for elevenses. Nothing open so press onto Bourgneuf, famous for its red Poitou-Charente wines, nothing open! I know Napoleon called us 'a nation of shopkeepers' but at least we open ours! Give up on elevenses and settle for my water bottle which is actually quite chaud now. Temperatures are in the early 30s today but at least the forecast for rain seems wrong.

After 40 uneventful miles, I reach Surgeres and stop for lunch. Brasserie is serving a plat du jour at €8 for three courses so after last night's lobster I say oui. Can't find the Stella Artois (are they hiding it I wonder?) so settle for coke and a large bottle of cooled water. Just finishing my poulet a la Bazaine, named after a French General who lost to the Germans in 1870 (don't they all, I whisper), when Royan Cycling Club roll in. Not one of them looks under 60 (men and women) and they are on a three-day randonee out of Royan. 'Where do you leeve,' one asks. In Eelkley, in God's own county, I say, showing them my Wednesday scarf. Looking suitably unimpressed, they shoot off over the horizon with a gallic humpf.

It's onward and eastward to my evening halt in Melle. Uneventful again, except for a snake (it was an adder, I think) crossing the road in front of me.

Melle, it turns out, is a fortified hilltop town so I face a steep climb up to the town square. I could do without it after 73 miles but that's life. After a bath and decision between the Cup Final or dinner, I opt for dinner.

Anyway, that's all folks, for now. Weather report is fine for tomorrow then rain for three days so I had better get the rain gear to the top of my pannier.

Oh, and Barcelona beat the Gooners. Why, oh why didn't Campbell crock Ronaldinho and for good measure Henry? Would have done our World Cup chances no end of good.

Quiz: Melle's claim to fortune is its mines. Founded by the Romans and hence the fortified town. What I want to know tonight is what were they mining that needed fortifying? One guess only please.

Off the Road

Lunch: Le Poulet Bazaine – chicken in a tomato and peppers sauce with tortellinis in a creamy mushroom sauce. Named after a French general. Surprisingly good, but then, I was famished. Followed by a French version of custard tart. Washed down with coke, water and espresso noisette. €8 all in.

Dinner: Les Glycines. A gastronomic restaurant in Melle and upstairs, my bed for the night. After a soak in the bath, I go for the menu decouverture. First up are three cheesy and anchovy flavoured puff pastry swirls. Very tasty. Then for pre-entrees, it's the smallest asparagus you have ever seen. 'Asperge jaune,' she says. Must be babies, I say. Like slivers, served with slivers of carrot and a white mousse which has essence of anchovy. Delightful!

Entrée – fois gras (paté) with little toasts with sultanas! And a glass of Pineau des Charente which is a bit like sweet sherry. Love the fois gras and sherry, not so keen on the sultanas.

Mains – magret de canard in spices served with fresh broad beans, new pots and carrots. Pretty good but nothing special. Should have had the pigeon with girolles!

Cheeses – getting full and dessert still to come so only pick five cheeses... only kidding, make it three. Rembouchon – hard and uninspiring; chevre – stunning, very strong; Pont L'Evec – the star, very strong!

Dessert – souffle of molten chocolate with vanilla ice cream. Say no more.

Wine – a bottle of Château Clement Pichon, a Cru Bbourgeois from the Haut-Médoc. Quite fine, delectable even. Reminds me of home or rather our cellar! All for €39 (excluding the wine) – not bad value eh?

The fortifications outside Saint-Martin de Re

The main gate into Saint-Martin de Re

The Pont Viaduc linking La Rochelle with the Isle de Re

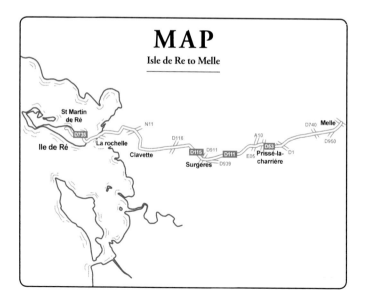

_Day 4

Date: 18 May 2006

57 miles

Left Melle at 9am. Little to report except that it's overcast and rain is forecast until Monday! La belle Francais! An uneventful morning as I do not see a soul in over an hour – France seems to be closed again! Stop in Gizay for elevenses, fancy a bun but the bar is bun free. Settle for a strong coffee noisette.

Press on for an early lunch in Gencay as I have a shorter day today to allow me time to tramp over the field of Poitiers where our Black Prince stuffed the flower of French nobility in 1356. Can't wait. Just as I reach the castle town of Gencay, it starts to rain. At least the wind is behind me today.

Find a lovely little Relais & Château underneath the castle walls for lunch. Wonder if the Black Prince stayed here on his tour in 1356? I order soupe de poissons and les pastas fraiche avec coquille St Jacques.

Head off, full of expectation to see the battlefield of Poitiers. Arrive in Noaille Murportois to find a convenient sign to Le Champ de Bataille. Carry on and on, and on and find pathetic field now taken over by itinerant French housewives growing veg. I ask about the memorial and get a vague look. Carry on for half a mile to find small memorial to 'La Reine de France et son soldats: 1356' and that's it. What a disappointment. Still, it was an English victory so perhaps if the roles were reversed, we might not take too kindly to putting up French monuments to French victories in Yorkshire. Impossible, I hear you say, they are rubbish swimmers and we had Nelson. Still, I hope to find better historical legacies at Tours tomorrow.

Off to the inn for the night to find it closed. Defer to local bar for a beer while it opens. After an hour, I ring them. 'It is closed,' they say. 'I know,' I say, 'I am outside and the doors are locked.' 'No, they say,' 'it is closed for the year.' 'What!!' I yell, or rather 'Quel!!'. 'Impossible, I booked two months ago'. 'C'est la vie,' she says. I bet the Black Prince didn't have to put up with this. It's probably revenge for 1356.

I decide to press onto Poitiers to hit the town. Must be busy as the first three hotels I find are full. Have to settle for sleazy two-star with no electricity. It will be back on shortly, he says! Have a bath and snooze, when suddenly the tele turns on by itself, and its on *Canal 9*! Hot stuff! Things are looking up.

Forgot to mention, the third of the usual three disasters to hit today is losing my sunglasses. They have been with me a long time – from Lands End to John O'Groats no less. Now they have a new home somewhere in Poitiers. Rain is forecast for next three days, so I won't miss them, sob sob. To compensate for the crappy hotel, I find Maximes, Poitiers finest restaurant. Fancy some boeuf tonight.

Quiz: And finally to today's question. The Black Prince was also the Prince of Wales. Who was his Dad and what special skill did the Welshmen have in his army? TTFN.

Off the Road

Lunch: Delightful stop by the castle at Gencay, Le Vieux Château. Start with soupe de poissons with all the trimmings. Excellente! Choose a 2003 Sancerre Rouge – just a half bottle of course. Main course is fresh pasta with scallops. Comes with lots of cream and with grated carrot on top with lettuce round the outside! At least there are no slices of orange! A little bland but I need the carbs so feast on the pasta. Finish with crème brulee with petals of honey. Which turn out to be corn flakes covered in honey! But very nice all the same.

Dinner: Maximes in Poitiers. Should have been at a nice little spot in St Benoit but the inn was closed, permanently. Supposedly the best in Poitiers.

Pre-starters – usual cheesy puff pastry things. Not as good as last night. And crispy bacon roll, but what is inside it? Tastes sweet and figgy? Not nice. Then a peach-coloured ice cream sorbet. But not peach, not sure what it is.

Entrée – raviolis with warm huitres and tomato. So so.

Mains – fillet de bouf with champignons and wrapped in pancetta. Pretty good but didn't like the pancetta.

Cheeses – finish with the 'chariot of cheese'. The best course by far. Oh, the Langue.

Wine – an Ampelidae 2003 from the Vienne. A local wine and new to me but very good all the same. Full bodied with lots of fruit and smooth on the palate. Chef came out to see what I thought. I said I liked the beef and cheese. Don't rush back.

The Battlefield at Poitiers, although less noisy than in 1356

Monument to the Queen of France at the Battle of Poitiers 1356

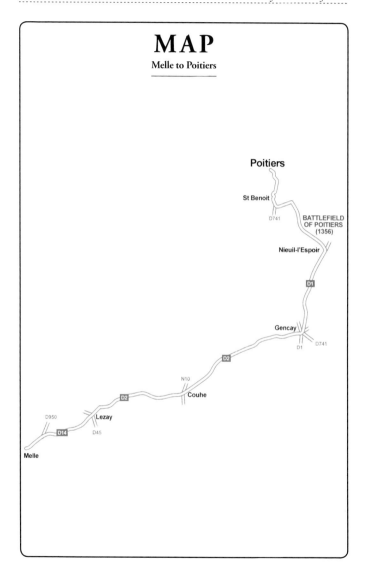

MAP

Melle to Poitiers

Poitiers

St Benoit

D741

BATTLEFIELD
OF POITIERS
(1356)

Nieuil-l'Espoir

D1

Gencay

D1   D741

D2

N10

Couhe

D2

D950   Lezay

D14   D45

Melle

_Day 5

Poitiers to Fontevraud L'Abbaye

Date: 19 May 2006   **69.5** miles

Restless night. Was bitten by mosquito in two-star Hotel Hell in Poitiers. After cheese sandwich for breakfast, head off with rain in the air. Today's highlight is the Battle of Tours 732 – I hope to have better luck than yesterday's battlefield quest! Inauspicious start by getting lost in Poitiers. Map in *Michelin Guide* is useless so fall back on Sat Nav. GPS picks up my position in seconds and shows I am heading in exactly the wrong direction! Turn around muttering insults to French road signage. Must have done five miles altogether before I find right road out of Poitiers.

Stop for elevenses in Dissay, a lovely moated château on the banks of the River Chain. Chaps in bar watching World Cup goals. None seem to be England so pretend to be French (i.e. humpf a lot and raise my eyebrows).

Amazingly, I find a signpost to the Champ de Bataille 732. But decide not to get too excited as this happened yesterday. Eventually, I see a small group ahead of me and hear someone giving a talk. 'Les Franks magnifique et les Arabiques miserable,' I hear. Must be the right place then. The French have done the battle proud with a diorama set out looking over the battlefield. Very informative. In a nutshell, the Battle of Tours was fought at Moussais 732. Abd El-Rahman with his Arab and Moorish army invaded France from Spain but was repulsed by Charles Martel with his Frankish army. Martel's son is Pepin the Short. His son was Charlemagne. Charles threw them out of Aquitaine and, as a result, not only do we not need to eat big sausages and wear funny shorts after the war, we also don't have to eat kebabs and slit the throats of our kids (that's the goats of course, not our children) in our lounges. Interesting eh?

Incidentally, the French call it the Battle of Poitiers? Perhaps to cover up their shattering defeat to us covered in yesterdays report? It is actually nearer to Châtellerault than to either Poitiers or Tours but its too hard to spell and has one of those funny lids on the A.

After a menu de jour at the local auberge, it's off for me. All being well, my next stop is the Abbey at Fontevraud, by the River Loire.

Unfortunately, the wind changes direction – against me – and starts to rain. Skies look dark so it's out with the heavy duty raingear. It takes more than a bit of rain to stop a Webster, although the lightning and thunder at Marennes nearly did it.

I rolled on through a small town where the entire population had assembled in the courtyard of the Mairie – turned out, there was a funeral on. I beat a hasty retreat hoping they were not still deciding whose funeral it was! They did look mafia-like but then the coffin came past me in a silver Ford Transit with big windows, like a Popemobile.

Finally arrived at Fontevraud at 6pm, wet and bedraggled. Delighted by welcome from receptionist who suggests she washes my cycling gear! Better wait until I take them off I say. Being British, I do that in the comfort of my own room, sans receptionist, I might add!

A delightful spot overlooking the River Loire. The hotel is called the Croix de Blanche and is a converted monastery next to the 12th Century Abbey. It has some famous residents... Richard the Lionheart, Henry II and Eleonor of Aquitaine are all buried here. I dine on smoked salmon, lamb sweetbreads and strawberry and rhubarb crumble. Only disturbed by Americans making their customary noise in the dining room! Walking Europe, one says to me. The Japs do it in air conditioned coaches I say.

On the cycling front, I have now completed over 370 miles and am one third of the way home. North of the Loire tomorrow and its back to the vineyards. What a shame!

Quiz: Today's questions go back to the Battle of Tours, or rather the Moors:

1) Who played the Moorish leader fighting Charlton Heston's El Cid outside the gates of Valencia? Incidentally, he also played Inspector Dreyfus in Beaky's favourite films.

2) Where was the last Arab stronghold in Spain before it was captured by Ferdinand and Isabella?

3) Charles Martel was honoured with a famous drink by the French. What type of drink is it?

Off the Road

Lunch: Small roadside auberge in Lencloitre (10 miles east of Châtellerault). Order plat du jour. Decline the buffet and await my poulet. Turns out to be a chicken leg, with a pyramid of rice and ratatouille. I cut off as much meat as I can find from the chicken and mix it up with the rice and rat. Actually quite good but I am hungry and need sustenance for the afternoon. Stilll have 40 miles to cover. Could do with a massage today as body seems to ache a bit. Expect I have no chance so it's mind over matter for me! Finish my house rosé and café noisette and set off again.

Dinner: At the Croix de Blanche in Fontevraud. A converted 12th-Century monastery next to an ancient abbey. A gorgeous hotel overlooking the River Loire. Got my cycling gear washed, now for dinner!

Entrée – home smoked salmon with kitchen herbs and sour cream. Not quite historic but close. Salmon very subtle with a matching dressing plus avocado and radish.

Mains – pan fried lamb sweetbreads with a bell pepper sauce. Sweetbreads (lambs balls) were fantastic but no bellpeppers and polenta chips instead! Hate Polenta so it took the edge off the meal.

Pudding – strawberry and rhubarb crumble with strawberry sorbet. Expectation better than the real thing. Crumble is good but needs custard not sorbet to make it really stand out. Oh for some Birds!

Wines – glass of Savennieres (blanc) which was quite perfumed but bold and oaky. A little like a Corton-Charlemagne, but only a little. Demi-Bouteille of Château de la Grille, from Chinon. Served quite cool for my liking but grew on me. Pleasant nose of acacias and fairly full bodied. With a hint of liquorice.

Field of Poppies north of Poitiers

Part of the display at the Battlefield of Tours

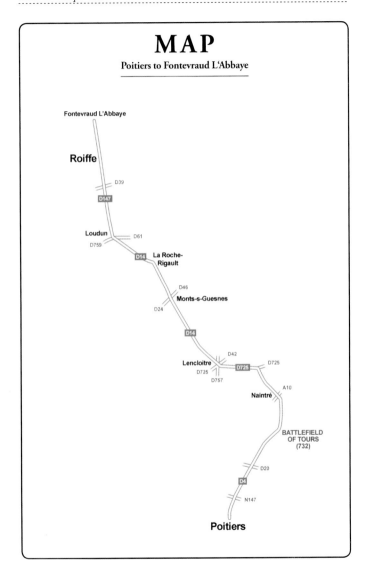

MAP

Poitiers to Fontevraud L'Abbaye

Fontevraud L'Abbaye

Roiffe

D39

D147

Loudun   D61

D759

D14   **La Roche-Rigault**

D46

Monts-s-Guesnes

D24

D14

D42

Lencloitre   D725

D725   D725

D757

A10

Naintré

BATTLEFIELD
OF TOURS
(732)

D20

D4

N147

Poitiers

Day 6 ——————— Fontevraud l'Abbaye to Loué

Date: 20 May 2006   **84.5** miles

Ah, day six and it is il pleut, tres pleut. 85 miles to do so I will have to break out the full rain monte. Shoe covers, leggings and raincoat. What a spree!

Head downhill to the river – La Loire – in all its damp and wet glory. Turn east to head downriver but against the wind. Feel twinge in right calf muscle. Going for a full set now – both hamstrings, groin and now calf. Expect it will be the back next, with only the neck and bum needed for a full set. Still I am nearly 50 and it is mind over matter!

Saumur is twinned with famous English castle town. Château used by Napoleon as a prison. Has some excellent wines – the glorious Sancerre among them. But it's too early so settle for coffee.

Passing wide of Le Mans to avoid the racers and all the hullaballoo that goes along with it. I can't get in my first choice hotel today because of them.

Press on and wind eases in the afternoon as I cross the Loir (not the same one, this is without the 'e' and is smaller, like a baby Loire) and the Sablé-sur-Sarthe. Busy little place, so stop for a beer.

Last 15 miles to Loué. Loué is about ten miles west of Le Mans and a motorbike race is taking place tomorrow on the famous circuit hence the hotel and all hotels around Le Mans are very busy. Loué is famous for only one thing, as far as I can tell, and I will be partaking later!! I cannot spoil the surprise now as it will be in the quiz.

A tough day today with 32mph winds predominantly from the east and unfortunately my first 20 miles was east before I turned north. Covered 85 miles and have now done over 450 miles in total. Tomorrow is a half day for me – it is a Sunday after all – only 38 miles to Alençon. I should be snoozing nicely in Normandy by early afternoon.

Can't finish without a mention in despatches for the Hotel Ricordeau at Loué, best meal so far.

Quiz:
1) What English castle town is Saumur twinned with?
2) What do Samurians grow in their caves?
3) Who drove the Porsche in the 1968 film *Le Mans*?
4) What is Loué famous for?

Off the Road

Lunch: Slumming it today after yesterday's lovely meal. Twix and Vittel will have to do. All restaurants, inns and auberges seem to be closed – on a Saturday! No one wants my Euros for a few frites!

Dinner: Hotel Ricordeau in Loué. A smart-looking hotel (a Logis de France) in a non-descript town. It is near Le Mans and it seems very busy as the famous race is on very soon – maybe this weekend. Turns out it's the bike race and not the famous car race. Nice gardens with a pool – too chilly, even for me. It's Saturday night and I didn't get any lunch so I intend to spoil myself tonight! So its the menu degustation for me!

Pre-starters – usual little crispy, cheesy thing with a bit of tuna and prawn with sour cream. Classy. Fois gras – small piece of sauted fois gras on a homemade chutney with what I thought were slivers of green beans but they tasted of curry! Not sure about them but loved the fois gras. Asparagus with Loué poussin eggs (it's what it's famous for!) – well, where to start! A boiled egg on top of crab meat in a pool of green pea veloute. And three asparagus spears. Gorgeous. When I broke the egg, it was runny and went all over the crab. It was different, but a great combination of flavours and the star of the show so far. And the egg was to die for, honest.

Langoustines – three very, I mean very tasty langoustines, each in its own potato pot! Three small new potatoes hollowed out with the langoustine inside. With yet another veloute, this time of bacon. Although there were no discernible pieces of bacon, it did indeed taste of bacon! Magnifique! Oh, and a few bits of cabbage for the rabbits. Star of the show so far!!

Lobster and sole – you are not going to believe it but the dishes just get better and better. Where to start? Three bite-size pieces of fried sole on a bed of mashed potatos, small glass of hot lobster bisque, lobster on top of Loué poussin (baby chicken) and to top it all, and a first for me, lobster sorbet to finish! Can you believe it? Truly historic and yes, the star of the show so far, although the lobster sorbet can be discarded.

Sweetbreads – yet again where to start, another beautiful dish. Lamb sweetbreads (actually taste a bit like liver but meatier) with gravy, two spring onions, baby carrots and spinach, couscous and fig chutney! Historic and maybe better than last night's sweetbreads in Fontevraud, but I will have to go with the lobster and sole and chicken dish as my favourite. Starting to feel a little weary now. I think the two Camparis and a bottle of wine are the culprits. Ah yes and 85 miles on a bike! Still always room for cheese, Gromit!

Cheese – well I never. Epoisse de Langue – hold your nose and feast your taste buds baby. And a very similarly strong cheese from Alsace and a brie. All brilliant but the Alsace was best. Yes, it even beat the Langue.

Puds – first up two sorbets, mango and rhubarb. Not just sorbet though, fresh mango and rhubarb in their own little pots with crème fraiche. I have to admit even I am getting full now! Main pud is pina colada! Juice, peppermint chocolate, passion fruit on coconut on tuille biscuit. Actually devine! I think that's it! Apart from café and petit fours. I'm stuffed can't even manage a wafer thin mint. Good job, I have a lie-in tomorrow!

Wines – Sancerre – classic, crisp and sharp with that gorgeous sweet finish on the palate. Bourgueil – Domaine de la Butte 2003. Proprietor Jacky Blot, would you believe. Nice colour, woody nose. Smooth on the palate and full-bodied. Not a Bordeaux but very good. All this and it doesn't even have a Michelin Star! I can't believe it, I really can't! Must come back.

The Château overlooking the River Loire at Saumur

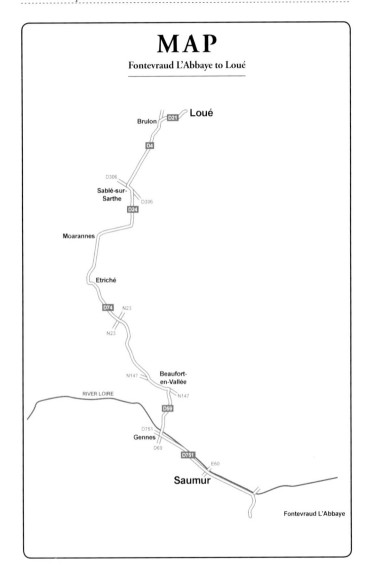

MAP
Fontevraud L'Abbaye to Loué

Loué

Brulon — D21

D4

D306

Sablé-sur-Sarthe

D306

D24

Moarannes

Etriché

D74 — N23

N23

N147 — Beaufort-en-Vallée

N147

RIVER LOIRE

D69

D751

Gennes

D69

D751 — E60

Saumur

Fontevraud L'Abbaye

_Day 7

Date: 21 May 2006

40 miles

7am – take one look out of window and make instant decision to have a lie in – it's pouring! It is Sunday morning after all and I only have 38 miles to cover. So it's back to sleep for me. Wake again at 8.30am and the rain has stopped so get up for breakfast. Feel remarkably fit and calves and hamstrings seem to have given up complaining.

Fancy Sunday morning fry up but have to settle for cornflakes and pain au chocolate. Leave at 10am with a tail wind heading north east to Normandy. Take an early elevenses in Silly (actually its Sillé le Guillaume) and contemplate last night's historic meal. It must go down as one of the top five meals of all time and I am still astonished it doesn't have a Michelin Star. I must have hit the chef on a great night or he had a bad one when the inspector called!

Anyway, for the record, here are my all-time top five meals (four of which are in France surprise, surprise):
1) Jean Bardet in Tours
2) Alain Ducasse's Louis XV in Monte Carlo
3) The Roux Brothers' Waterside Inn in Bray near Windsor
4) Corbeillan Bages in Pauillac
5) Hotel Ricordeau in Loué

Also for the record my top five in the UK are:
1) The Roux Brothers' Waterside Inn in Bray
2) Eric Chavot at the Capital Hotel, London
3) The Winteringham Arms near the Humber Bridge
4) The Summer Isles Hotel in Achiltibuie
5) Lobster with linguini at Zafferanos in London

It must be very right wing round here as lots of 'Le Pen pour le Président' posters. Stop for a beer for lunch. A light lunch today, beer and Bounty bars. Arrive in Alençon at 3pm after finally covering 40 miles today. Alençon has a surprisingly pretty medieval centre with the proverbial Notre Dame church. No one in at the hotel but owner has given me the code number to let myself in! Its 2062 but don't tell anyone. Bit grotty after last two nights. Need to find a restaurant open on a Sunday night in provincial french town. Now that will be a challenge! Still, I saw a Chinese on my way into town so could always fall back on a take-away back in my hotel room.

No quiz today – it's Sunday – but don't forget to send me your all-time top five restaurants.

Another week to come and another 500 miles!

Off the Road

Lunch: Beer and Bounty bars in Fresnay. After last night, I need a breather!

Dinner: After the Lord Mayor's Show! Nothing of note open in Alençon on a Sunday night. Eventually, find little Italian retaurant, Le Napoli. Looks tidy enough and order spag bol with half a bottle of Chianti. What a mistake... disgusting, tinned tomatoes and gristly mince. Beat a hasty retreat. Hopefully, normal service will be resumed tomorrow.

Fresnay sur Sarthe west of Le Mans

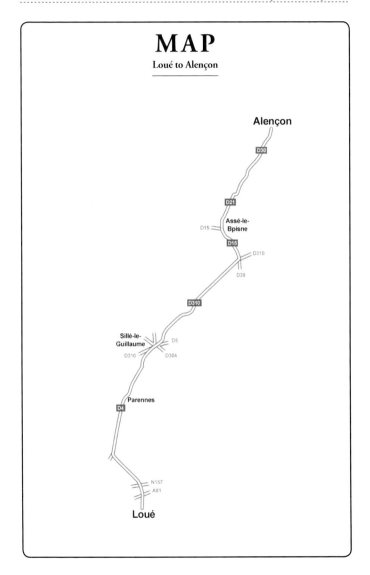

MAP
Loué to Alençon

Alençon

D30

D21

Assé-le-
Bpisne

D15

D15

D310

D39

D310

Sillé-le-
Guillaume

D5

D310

D304

Parennes

D4

N157

A81

Loué

_Day **8**

Date: 22 May 2006   **90.5** miles

7am on a wet, windy and cold Monday morning in Alencon. But no luxury of a lie-in this morning as I have 82 miles to cover. Plus head a little heavy after night on the beer with bikers. OK, you are asking, what was I up to? Well, you will recall, I am near to Le Mans. Well, all the motor bikers I was seeing yesterday were visiting for the Grand Prix at Le Mans. Many were English and some of them were staying in Alencon last night. I was enjoying the news coming in via *Yahoo!* that Leeds were losing the play-off final and so popped across the road for a quick beer to celebrate before bed. Well, it was full of English motorbikers partying before they travelled back home on Monday. I said I too was a biker and, when I shared my news about Leeds, I was taken into the fold, so to speak. They were mainly from Norwich, of all places. Anyway, they let me go in the late, or was it early, hours. You can imagine their surprise in the morning when they saw 'my bike'! Where's the engine they said? I pointed to my thighs. I put on my rain gear as they slapped on the leathers. If only I had an engine, I would be an honorary member of the Norwich Hells Angels now!

Set off wet, bothered and bewildered (name that song) but with a south westerly to push me along. Then, after 12 miles, disaster! Get first puncture just outside Essay. Back wheel as ever and in a howling gale. Decide to take no chances by fitting new 'puncture-resistant inner tube'. Back on road in 30 minutes but tube must be twisted as its a bit bumpy. Stop in Moulin where very nice homme in Renault garage lets me use his air pump. Fix tube and get 100psi in so it's normal service resumed and storm into Aigle at 18mph for lunch. Fancy omelette and chips but definitely no beers!

With the wind in my sails, I flew through the Forest de Breteuil at 18mph. Only drawback, another downpour. Arrived in pretty market town of Breteuil in need of a pick me up. A glass of Port, a coffee and a Bounty bar does the trick.

Breeze past Evreux and downhill to the River Eure. Only problem is, I have to climb out of the river valley on the other side and it looks steep! I could do without it after covering almost 90 miles today. True enough the climb from Menille is 1 in 5! Toughest climb of the trip so far but I make it with a rest halfway up. Three more miles and reach the Château de Brecourt. A Louis XIII-style château that claims to be a 'Hotel of Distinction'.

Covered 90.5 miles today at an average speed of 13.2 and a max speed of 39.8. Now over halfway in miles at 587.5. I am the nearest I get to Paris tonight but can't quite see the Eiffel Tower.

Some interesting replies to yesterday's survey on favourite restaurants. The Jazz and Cigar club in Tokyo? Keep them coming in.

One more solid days cycling and I start the battlefields again. Whoopee.

Quiz: Who played Louis XVII, or was it XVIII, in the 1970 film *Waterloo*? And to whom Marshall Ney said 'Sire, I will bring that monster back in a cage'. Who was he referring to?

Off the Road

Lunch: Aigle. Omelette and frites in town inn. Not bad but cheese a bit gooey. Saving myself for tonight.

Dinner: Château de Brecourt, near to Vernon (30 miles west of Paris). Beautiful hotel/château but only seems to be me here! Setting some more tables for dinner but they must be late. It is 8.30pm now. I avoid the menu degustation tonight and go with a simple fish combination but with a chocolate surprise at the end! Pre-starter of crème de carrot. Served piping hot and devine actually.

Entrée – lobster, and Breton lobster no less. Half of one anyway! Served cut but returned to the shell with some gorgeous dark brown splodges on the plate (which incidentally is a rectangle of black slate!). Dark splodges contain dijon mustard. Also some green stuff – left that!

Mains – small goujons of sole (not battered I might add) in a large puff pastry case – almost a vol-au-vent for a giant! With a grey tartare sauce and squid ink perhaps and girolles. And, nearly forgot baby carrots. Has to be one of THE BEST fish dishes I have ever had. Historic. Magnifique. What else can I add. I want you all to try it! Am I getting carried away? I should cha cha.

Cheeses – two local cheeses: Pont le Vec and Rochambeau, and the old favourite,

Langue. Langue not as good as at Hotel Ricordeau. Pont le Vec is strong but salty. Rochambeau OK. Overall, they are too cold. Just out of the fridge perhaps? OK, but no great shakes.

Pudding – le chocolat in three parfums with chantilly praline and warm churros. Like a large chocolate mousse with three layers for each flavour. Starting on the top with a creamy one. Then a stronger one, then at the bottom the business – full on baby! With two sugafy churros to dip in. Very good!

Wine – white – Sancerre from Saumur. Brings back memories... of rain! Served at a perfect temperature, i.e. not too cold. Delightful. Red – a 1998 St Estephe. That certain Bordeaux nose and what a taste! That old red magic has me in its spell every time. Overall, it lacked atmosphere. I was the only diner on a Monday night – but that sole dish will live long in the memory.

The dining room at the Château de Brecourt near Douains. Only me at the Inn!

Miserey, and it was in the rain, just east of Evreux

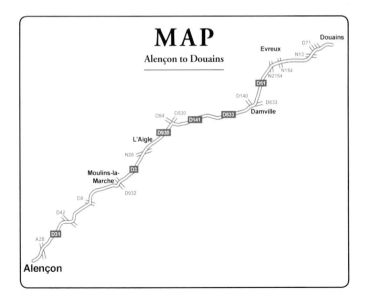

_Day 9

Douains to Aumale

Date: 23 May 2006   **71** miles

Stopped for early bird coffee in Vernon on the banks of the Seine. Funny old place France, even when its busy, nobody is doing much! Weather much better today, cracked open the suntan lotion for first time in many days. Oh. La belle France!

Crossed the Seine and the Epte and followed the west bank of the Epte northwards. Beautiful countryside interspersed with numerous châteaux. Aveny was particularly spectacular. Interestingly, for you bikers and as you know I am now an honorary member of the Norwich Hells Angels, I passed through Gasny which is twinned rather unusually with an English town. Watch later for the quiz question.

Then arrived in Bordeaux Ste Claire, for elevenses – I always knew you were special Claire! Now I know you are the Saint of Bordeaux! And even more intriguing is that Ste Claire is in the commune of Ste Claire sur Epte. Which, as you know, is an anagram of Pete! Strange.

Onto Gisors for lunch. Not as pretty as I expected so I bought a tuna sandwich and sat by the river. Too cold to swim though as it has gone ominously dark. Yes, two minutes later and it buckets it down. Repare to nearest tree avec tuna sarnie and pray there is no lightning!

Now back in heavy duty rain gear, I am off again. Unfortunately, I seem to have picked the main route to Dieppe and it's full of lorries, mainly Polish for some reason and its not Pledge! Decide on plan B to get to Gournay via back roads and meet the local Citroen Deux Chevaux rally club on their weekly outing. Too slow, so overtake them and zoom into Gournay for my afternoon glass of Port.

The last 20 miles to Aumale for my overnight stop is blighted by frequent showers. Consequently, I seem to be stopping every five minutes to put my raincoat on! Pretty countryside through the Pays de Bray though and in fine weather it would be a treat. Just south of the Forest of Eu, Aumale is a small place (2,577 inhabitants last time they counted). It does host however the Villa des Houx, my hotel for the evening. Tomorrow brings two treats but more of these tomorrow!

Quiz: Which English 'circuite de racing' town is twinned with Gasnay?

Off the Road

Lunch: A tuna sandwich and coke sitting by the riverbank in Gisors. Finished with two 'financiers' and a shortbread biccie – or rather two shortbread biccies with a thick layer of chocolate in between! Now where's that suntan oil?

Dinner: Villa des Houx, Aumale. Sort of an Elizabethan-looking building on the outside. Insided two-star and modern, but clean and cosy. Restaurant looks the best room so I hope their food is their ace card! It is! And I'm in heaven. They have a menu choice totally dedicated to lobster. Would you believe it! So I order it with a glass of Chardonnay and a half bottle of Louis Latour Cote de Beaune 2000 (I'm cutting down don't you know tonight!). The head waiter takes some convincing that I should have red wine with my lobster but I hold firm for the red. Those Frenchies, they are so old fashioned... but I like them!

Before the start the head waiter (who looks like a German) brings me my lobster to appraise. Still alive, I stroke its back before it goes in the pot. It does look rather small though to stretch across 3 courses! Au revoir, I say, as he takes it away, as I will be seeing it again, it will just be rather pinker next time!

La Soupe Glace de Homard at concombre – turns out to be cold cucumber soup with a generous dollop of lobster mousse and a lobster claw. Very good and I even liked the cold cucumber soup. Le Ravioli de Homard – one very big ravioli stuffed with lobster together with a warm lobster sauce, the other lobster claw, and those darned baby asperges again. Gorgeous they are, and the lobster.

Le Sorbet Calvados – not with any lobster in it! Shame. I had lobster sorbet the other night at the Ricordeau. Wow, what a meal that was! It could use some lobster, worse course yet. Like frozen apple sauce with a kick. Never was good with sorbets. Bring back my lobster! Bring back my lobster!

La Queue de Homard en Papillote – well, en papillote means poached in a silver foil bag. Cut open at my table. Magnifique, and came with yellow rice (not bad), broccoli (ugh) and braised fennel (so so).

Le Fromage – not a chariot today alas but a tray. Pick Pont le Vec again (after last night), Neufchatel (the local) and mauvoise (never heard of it but looks good). Star of the show is the Neufchatel. Really creamy, salty but with a wicked tang!

Le dessert – crepes á la orange. At last, pancakes! And they are on fire! Classic dish cooked to perfection.

Overall – a lovely homage to le homard! Spoiled only yet again by loud Americans

Château de Brecourt at Douains

Château de Baudemont near Bray on the banks of the River Epte

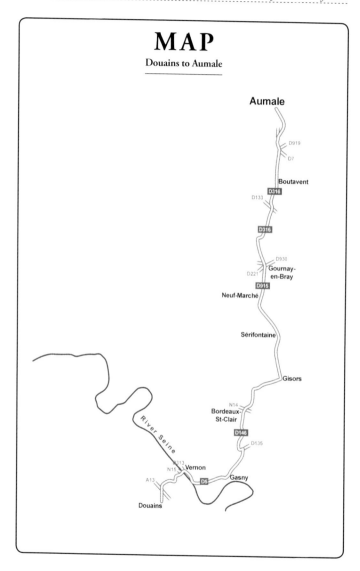

MAP

Douains to Aumale

_Day **10**

Date: 24 May 2006

70 miles

Funny thing I noticed last night chatting to the locals in the bar. They saw me arrive 'a velo' but not one person apart from the Canadian outside Pauillac has asked me about my journey! Not sure if it's the French reserve or politeness not to inquire into one's personal business. Two years ago, on my Lands end to JOG trip, nearly everyone I met asked me about my trip! Maybe my French is worse than I thought.

Anyway, the business in hand. It's Crecy day today! Plus as a special treat: Château de Montreuil for dinner – 1 Michelin star!

So take yourselves back to 1346, ten years before Poitiers and Edward III is falling back towards the Channel Ports with a large French and Bohemian army on his tail. Blind King John leads the Bohemians – how I'm not quite sure without Sat Nav! The Black Prince, only a teenager in 1346, leads the King's (his father) right wing.

This is the scene then as I head for Abbeville but first a steep climb out of the Bresle River valley. Steepest and longest climb yet, but the legs are well toned now and I get up in one go. Reward is a coffee and KitKat in Oisement. Then onto cross the Somme (not for the first time this trip) at Abbeville for an early lunch.

Pleasant ride through the Forêt de Crécy brings you to Crécy-en-Ponthieu itself. Unprepossessing town but find sign to Champ de Bataille. A small display is set out beneath a look-out tower that replaces the moulin used by Edward III during the battle to watch the French approach. The moulin was unceremoniously burnt down by outraged Frenchmen in 1898 following the Fashoda Incident. The English men at arms in two divisions under Northampton and the Black Prince were aligned on the ridge sweeping back to Wadicourt with their longbowmen ranged in front. The French under Philip VI of Valois approached from Abbeville. Among their number was blind King John Luxembourg King of Bohemia.

The dastardly French are soaked just prior to the battle and when they send their Genoese crossbowmen forward, they get the full glare of the sun in their eyes making them very cross! All this a sure sign that God is on our side. Our archers let loose and force the Genoese to withdraw. This precipitates a charge by the French knights who mow down the remaining Genoese (not a good battle for the Genoese who are killed in equal numbers by both sides) and head for the English lines. However, they get stuck in the mud in the valley bottom and are mercilessly hit by arrows from our archers. Eventually, Edward ordered forward his men at arms who finish off the French as they flounder in mud trapped beneath their horses.

After the battle, Edward orders all his men that can write to make a list of the French knights killed. Hence, it is now known as the Valley of the Clerks. I wondered how they knew their names and then I realised. They use the 'school borders' system. They had name tags on! When you think about it, when the French army are camped up for the night eating frogs legs and quaffing Calvados, what do they do with their armour? They take it off and pile it up, of course. So, the next morning when they pile out of their tents looking for an iron shirt how do they find their one? With engraved name tags they can instantly spot their armour and in a jiffy they are ready to slaughter English knaves. Problem solved.

Among the dead was blind King John. The clerks knew him as he was the only knight strapped to his horse carrying a white stick instead of a sword!

Poor old King Philip was wounded in the thigh and neck and retreated to ease his wounds. Hence, the phrase 'pain in the neck'.

After the battle, I continue north (liked Edward) and stop overnight in Montreuil. Good job because the wind is picking up and heading straight for me. Hope it clears for tomorrow as I have another famous English victory not 22 miles away!

Quiz: Today it may be a little harder:
1) What links Prince Charles to the Battle of Crecy and why can he be truly said to be a 'Bohemian'?
2) Why was Montreuil famous during the First World War?
Get on Google or preferably get your thinking caps on!

Off the Road

Lunch: Abbeville. Sat in the square with a sandwich and beer (ham and cheese) and read *The Times*. Starts to rain, so head indoors for a noisette. Fancy a Port but decide to wait until later.

Dinner: Château de Montreuil. The weather is bloomin' awful so I will cheer myself up with the seven course menu degustation at this wonderful Michelin-starred establishment (I've been before!). Plus, I have lost exactly 1 stone (down to 11st 10lb now) so I think I deserve it.

First course – starting at the bottom reading up – raw tuna (carpaccio), sort of tuna mayo/cucumber mix, two big oysters, red caviar. Wonderful!

Second course – red mullet on a pesto and red pepper sauce on top of a small piece of toast. But the surprising bit is a pot of vanilla ice cream floating on olive oil! Actually, brilliant! Loved it. The fish was very tender and melted in the mouth.

Third course – fresh asparagus lightly sauted with small pieces of Parma ham, then two shitake mushrooms in a reduction on top of the tiniest tortellinis you have ever seen! Quite simply staggeringly effective. Wonderful mixture of flavours and I am quickly becoming an asparagus fan.

Fourth course – who used to say 'I can't believe it'? Well, I can't believe it. I was thinking that I've not had beef yet for dinner on this tour. When what turns up? You guessed it, lamb... no, I'm joking, it's beef. Fillet to be exact with fois gras on a bed of baby carrots on the side with a roast potato shaped like a rose and with my own little silver jug of gravy! A masterpiece. I could eat it again!

Fifth course – a warm tart – about time I say! Turns out to be cheesy though so decline in favour of 'La Chariot'.

Sixth course – fresh cherries to dip in vanilla emulsion, then bits of pistachio and finally chocolate sauce. Devine. I want more!

Seventh course – well, another pud! Millefeuille of raspberries and cream with sorbet and some little green leaves that at first I think are mint but then realise they are aniseed. I have officially run out of superlatives now. What more can I say? Out of this world.

Wines – a glass of Sancerre (decide not to go for two bottles of red and white tonight!) to start. Château Haut Marbouzet 2000 – a classic red from a favourite St Estephe vineyard. Deep red colour, true Bordeaux nose and it lies in the mouth like velvet. A class act if ever I have drunk one, and I have. Must get some for my cellar although I'm pretty sure I have some 1986 which should be really swinging now!

Overall – as you know, I have been here before. The menu was different (I guess they feature what is fresh at the time) but this is how I summed it up back then. 'Well its a 9! A top score. I'll have to bring you to this one! A magical meal – must try the cheese trolley next time!' So there you have it. Two magical meals. And, if anything it was better this time. Almost creeping into my all-time top five. And I've still not brought you here! Darlings, I must get you in the diary!

Display at the Battlefield of Crecy

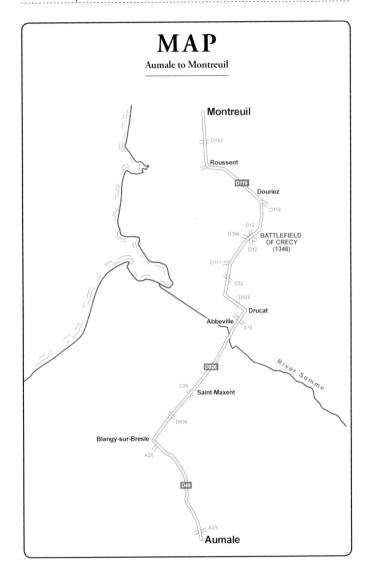

MAP

Aumale to Montreuil

Montreuil

D142

Roussent

D119

Douriez

D119

D12

D398

BATTLEFIELD
OF CRECY
(1346)

D12

D111

D32

D926

Drucat

Abbeville

A16

River Somme

D926

D29

Saint-Maxent

D936

Blangy-sur-Bresle

A28

D49

A29

Aumale

_Day 11 —————— Montreuil to Arras

Date: 25 May 2006 **66** miles

What a surprise. As I look out of my bedroom window, it's cold, wet and raining. So much for hot sunny days on tour in France. May as well do Iceland next trip!

One bright spot today is Agincourt. Back to 1415 and King Henry V is beating a hasty retreat back to the Channel Ports, much like me! And I am visiting the field where it happened today.

Decide its time for serious wet gear today. Shoe covers, winter socks, rainproof trousers over cycling shorts and Mont Maison Extreme over my base layer and cycling shirt. That's a Berghaus Extreme by the way! With all that and my helmet, I almost feel like a French knight. So it's off to Agincourt.

After 10 miles down the Arthe, I stop for much needed coffee. Two bikers arrive, Hells Angels by the looks of them (one has horns on his helmet). I depart with a 'Je suis une Hells Cherub. Je n'ai pas une enjeane' comment.

I arrive in Azincourt, as it is now called, probably much like Henry V in 1415, wet and bedraggled but spirits raised by museum sign ahead. Museum is surprisingly good with helpful staff, models, animatronics, a show about the battle and, of course, lots of armour and weapons. What is amusing to me is that there is all this to commemorate an 'English' victory on French soil! I can't imagine it in England or perhaps not, thinking of Hastings – does that count as a 'French' victory on our soil or is that a Norman victory? The French staff look a bit gruesome (big and hairy) and that's when I realise who in their right minds would want to work here if they were French? The answer is that they are inmates from the local prison at Hesdin. The lucky ones get to break rocks, the rest have to work here every day looking at smirking English faces come to gloat!

I leave the museum complete with map to view the battlefield. The French numbering about 20,000 to 25,000 under D'Albret, Constable of France, are blocking Henry's route on the road back to Calais. It's a bit surprising the French King decided to stay in bed that day and send his constable instead. Bit like us sending Dixon of Dock Green to lead our army! Perhaps after Crecy and Poitiers, he thought better of it. Plus, the majority were Armagnacs, clearly inebriated most of the time! Anyway, Henry assembled his men opposite the French, numbering only 6,000 to 8,000. The English were clearly very anxious, if not down right scared to bits! The two sides stared at each other for four hours before Henry decided he had to make a move. The ground itself was pretty flat unlike the advantage Edward had at Crecy. However, as at Crecy, there had been a storm overnight causing the field to become very muddy. Ah ah, I can here you say, God has come to our aid once more! Henry moved his line 400 yards towards the French which brought his archers in reach of the French. The rain of arrows infuriated the Constable and he ordered his knights to charge the archers flanks. However, the mud bogged them down and they were decimated by the arrows. The French men at arms however were making progress in the centre, pushing back Henry's vanguard and killing the Duke of York (after the battle, his body was boiled to strip away his flesh so his bones could be sent back to England!). The decisive moment arrived when the archers, having routed the French cavalry, put down their bows, picked up knives and hatchets and fell on the French from both sides. In the mud, in heavy armour, the French were at a big disadvantage against the mobile archers. And crammed into so small a space they could not manoeuvre their weapons. It became a massacre.

The third wave of the French army retreated and Henry became immortal with a great victory. His route to Calais lay open and he returned to England a hero.

After two hours in the museum and mulling over the battlefield, I feel a little rumble in my stomach. Must be time for lunch. Lunch stop is St Pol sur Ternoise twinned, believe it or not, with Hebden Bridge in Yorkshire – almost feels like home! I struggle to find anything open and then, when I ask a stray gendarme, he tells me it's a Bank Holiday! Thursday 25 May – what a day to choose for a Bank Holiday? Only in France! Isn't it every other Thursday they take off? Anyway, find a brasserie open and after very nice steak and frites, it's off to my overnight stop, Arras. A nice run, with little wind, unlike yesterday and apart from the odd shower, the rain holds off.

Arrive in Arras at 5.30pm. The rain is still holding off and the place by the large Abbey (St Vaast) is full of people. Seems a bit incongruous in that the place is surrounded by tacky shops and bars. Very noisy as people in fancy dress spill out of the bars. Main theme seems to be The Blues Brothers and Nuns! I buy an ice cream (don't know why, I'm bloomin' freezing) and watch. Retreat to quiet of the Place de la Croix Rouge where my room for the night can be found. The L'Univers Hotel with its magnificent Le Clusius restaurant. Now, what shall I have tonight?

I forgot to give you my mileages yesterday. Today, I have covered 66 miles at an average speed of 11.7 mph. In total, I have covered 794.5 miles or approx 70% of my expected total on the trip. That's it for now folks. Back to the trenches for me tomorrow.

Quiz: You will all know already who directed the 1944 film *Henry V*. And, of course, who starred in it in the title role. I also want to know in which films did he speak these lines? 'Is it safe', 'What do they know of heaven or hell Cathy... if they know nothing of life?', 'A Thracian against a Nubian is always an interesting contest'. For a bonus, who spoke his lines in a scene added to the restored version of the last film after his death?

Off the Road

Lunch: Restaurant de Poste in St Pol sur Ternoise – grilled fillet with frites and mustard. Excellent meat and frites like frites should be. With a carafe of house red and a bottle of water. Coffee to finish.

Dinner: Restaurant Le Clusius, Hotel L'Univers, Arras. Hotel (a Best Western – no guarantee of class!) is in a quiet square away from the hustle and bustle of town. Originally a monastery and then a hospital in the war (1914 to 1918), it is now a hotel. An unexpected delight. Chef Herve Mit wanted me to taste his Spring menu.

Smoked Salmon – he wanted me to have his asperges but after the last two nights, I fancied something else. The salmon is sliced at the table so that sealed it. And it's excellent too. Can just overhear Americans on next table. Mum and dad and daughter with her husband. Mum has the fresh asperges. She queries their colour.

These are white, she says, back home ours are green? Daughter says 'here in Holland, that's how they grow them.' Hello!! What planet am I on? Get me off please. P.S. I don't need to hear them to know they are Yanks. The women are twice as wide as the men! Ooh, what a bitch I am tonight!

Veal sweetbreads with crawfish mousse potatoes and truffle – not what I expected. Came in a stewing pot with a lid on. Inside it looks messy but tastes ok. A crayfish head adorns the mashed potatoes. Struggle to find the meat bits but do eventually. Sauce is tasty and covers two large calf balls! Sorry, but you can't put too fine a point on it! Think I've done sweetbreads to death after this. Overall, okay but no veg apart from a mushroom and a tomato. Cheese – pretty poor art from the Langue.

Wines – white – a glass of Chardonnay from the Bourgogne. Sharp and not too sweet. Red – a half bottle of Château Tour de Pez 2001. The best part of the meal by a mile. A beautiful St Estephe.

Overall – well, I've been spoilt after the last few nights. Even so, it was not great. Just okay. Plus the staff were poor. Not enough of them (must be down to the Bank Holiday) and made too many gaffes: Campari served with tonic instead of soda; only one black pepper mill and it was on another table when my salmon arrived. The waitress refused to get it for me – I suggested she try harder!; bottle of wine left unopened when my main course arrived. Still. Maybe you need meals like this to appreciate the very good ones?

Rather wooden archers at the Battlefield of Agincourt

Just finished my ice cream in the main square at Arras

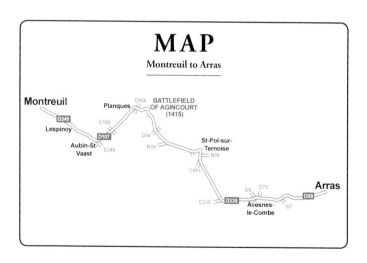

_Day 12 —————Arras to Ligny-en-Cambresis

Date: 26 May 2006   **64** miles

Well, I said it was back to the trenches for me today and I meant it literally. To the First World War trenches on the Somme to be exact. I aim to find the spot where the Sheffield City Battalion (my home town for those not aware) were decimated in 1916.

The weather is, as ever, decidedly dodgy but looking dry if very overcast. Not like 1 July 1916 which was very warm and sunny. Spoke too soon, heading south through beet fields, it starts to rain and heading into the wind, I do well to average 9 mph.

Spot first war graves eight miles south west of Arras. The Bucquoy Road Cemetery. Then at Gommecourt, the cemetery looks over the ground where the 46th Division attacked. At this point, 12 Battalions attacked one German Battalion. But only a few got through the barbed wire, machine gun fire and artillery shells to reach the German trench. It's sobering to read the register of names in the cemetery. No Websters but there is a Wells, a machine gunner. Stop in Hebuterne for a sobering cup of coffee.

What strikes you most about the Somme is the sheer scale of the area over which the battle was fought. The Somme itself is many miles to the south and the area over which the fighting took place stretches for about 30 miles. Briefly, the battle itself was supposed to be a diversion, to help the French, hard pressed at Verdun, by drawing German troops west. Lord Haig, new Commander in Chief of the British and Commonwealth army, committed about 100,000 troops to the attack on that fine July day. By the end of which, 60,000 were casualties, 21,000 dead. The worst day in our Army's history. Hardly any ground was taken and entire communities were decimated.

The Sheffield Battalion attacked near the village of Serre together with the Accrington Pals, the Burnley Pals and the Barnsley Pals. As the Sheffielders arrived looking very smart with their hankies tucked into their shirt cuffs, the Barnsley Pals said, 'look at the fancy dans from Sheffield, the coffee and bun boys!' I've never heard of Sheffield lads referred to as 'coffee and bun' boys before, usually it's more earthy. Needless to say, when the attack went in, it was a disaster, most are buried here and never had the chance to take coffee and buns in Sheffield again. The graves are tended with loving care by the War Graves Commission and the woods nearby are now called Sheffield Park.

You soon start to see more of the little dark green signs pointing out war graves as you continue along what was once the front line. There are literally dozens of them almost in every town and village.

Next along the route is Beaumont Hamel. This is where the Newfoundland Regiment attacked. Preserved beautifully with the trenches and shell holes, together with a superb museum, it is tended by work experience students from Canada who lead guided tours of the battlefield.

And then Thiepval. The Germans thought it one of the strongest positions along the whole 400 miles of the Western Front. They could not believe anyone would attack here! But, of course, we did. The Thiepval monument is immense and contains inscribed on its walls the names of all the soldiers who gave their lives at the Somme. Of course, many more were never found or identified, marked by 'Known unto God' graves, these are perhaps the saddest sights here. And I find the Websters, quite a few, and one from the Sheffield Battalion. Wonder if my gran knew him. She was 20 at the time, packing shells in Sheffield. The museum itself is very impressive with film shows and displays. What was interesting were the number of coaches rolling up on a regular basis with French school children. We should bring our school children here too. I think of my own Tom, flying over my head today on his way to Paris with school. He would learn something far more valuable in the long term by coming to Thiepval than visiting EuroDisney.

This place must surely be the definitive testament to man's inhumanity to man. And his stupidity. Pray it won't happen again.

Before I realise it, I have missed lunch. Didn't leave the War Museum at Thiepval until after 2pm. So hightailed it through the rain towards Cambrai and stopped in Metz.

Arrived in Ligny en Cambresis, about 10 miles south east of Cambrai at 5pm. Has a Michelin Star this one so should be back to form after last night.

Now last night's quiz only had one correct set of answers from Claire and Pete. Now vying with Graham and Jules for the supreme title with only five days left. Of course, the winners get a signed copy of my new book when published later in the year. Wow, I hear you say!

My last thoughts before I go to sleep tonight are that war is hell. There is no glory in war, just pain, suffering and death. We should make all our kids come here.

Quiz:
1) Who financed, produced and starred in the very famous 1957 black and white film of the horror of the First World War?
2) Who was the director?
3) What was the name of the film?
4) Who played the German Field Marshall in the film which took its title from Germany's highest decoration for pilots in the First World War?
5) What was the nickname given to Britain's first tank used for the first time on the Somme?

Off the Road

Lunch: Stopped in Metz for coffee, Porto, Mars bar and box of nuts.

Dinner: Le Château de Ligny en Cambresis. A XIII century château and a Michelin-starred menu! So its le menu prestige for me then.

A sort of Elizabethan-style dining room – all wood panelling and red wallpaper and a large chandelier hangs above my head. Oh, and a large wooden fireplace with two busty ladies carved in the sides.

Only one other table occupied so far. By very well-spoken late middle-aged English couple. Is that me... am I late middle-aged? I tell a lie, there is a large party on a table round the corner, with children. And then a chap comes in wearing a bow tie with his wife, I trust! P.S. He has a shirt and trousers on also.

Also, just looked down to my left and realise I have a little wooden chair for my handbag. Drat, if only I'd not left it in my room! The lady with the bow tie is using hers...Bitch!

First course – hot fois gras on a bed of cold green beans, slivers of carrot and, I think, slivers of turnip. Plus three small slices of potato. Works surprisingly well.

As you know, I don't normally do hot and cold together but this is quite good. Fois gras tastes splendid.

Second course – three oysters, warm, and out of their shells on top of asparagus, on top of creamed leeks. Divine!! The asparagus is sort of teenager size now. Not the babies like before, not the adults like the Yanks had yesterday but in between. All the same, bloody brilliant.

Third course - Breton lobster ravioli with diced courgettes served with a carapace of lobster sauce. Unbelievable! Sauce not creamy like most shellfish sauces. More like a gravy. Much, much better than the lobster ravioli at Le Villa des Houx.

Fourth course – pigeon breast, with a pistachio coating, served with pigeon wing and crispy skin, creamed potatoes and artichoke. A star course, particularly liked the crispy skin! Unlike me, eating fat! Picked up the bone and had a suck. Heaven.

Fifth course – it's cheeses from the 'chariot'. I select Epoisse de Langue, something strong in Calvados, and two others that look nice. The Epoisse is fantastic. Not so keen on the others.

Sixth course – raspberry sorbet – so so.

Seventh course – pineapples Victoria. Braised pineapple with panna cotta and waffles. Very good but I think I have reached saturation point now.

Wines – white – a Riesling from Alsace, a 1997 Hugel no less (the best apart maybe for some of the Australians). Gorgeous, that unmistakeable Granny Smith nose. And crisp, tart and long fruity finish. I do love Hugel! Red: a 2003 Bandol from Provence, a Domaine de Simone. Felt like a change from Bordeaux and I am no Rhône or Burgundy fan so went south to Provence. Not as full-bodied or dense as a Bordeaux but very palatable all the same. Second thoughts, perhaps I should have gone for the Branaire Ducru 1998!

Very, very good. But if pressed I would have to plump for Château de Montreuil ahead of the Château de Ligny in the battle of the Michelin stars. But not by much.

I fear this will be the last of my degustation reports as I head into Belgium tomorrow. It's mussels and frites after that!

The front line at Beaumont Hamel

Monument to the Newfoundlanders at Beamont Hamel

Gommecourt Wood Cemetery

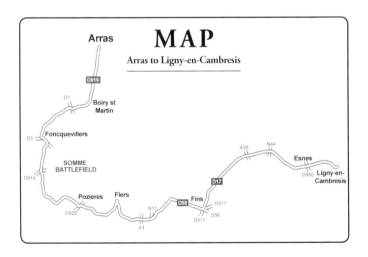

_Day 13 ——————— Ligny-en-Cambresis to Mons

Date: 27 May 2006   **54.5** miles

Still feel somewhat sombre after yesterday. So have an extra hour in bed. Then five minutes to contemplate crossing the border into Belgium. That's more than enough for contemplation of Belgium!

Breakfast throws up a surprise. There is omelette on the menu. After all these days of croissants and bits of baguette! I go for cornflakes – damn their impudence and don't want them to make a habit of it .

Set off at a leisurely pace as I only have about 50 miles to do to Mons over the border. Unfortunately after 10 miles and just outside Le Cateau, I get my second puncture, in the front though this time. Which is good because after 20 minutes I am back on board and ready for coffee in Le Cateau. Which is very famous for two of her sons, Mortier is one (one of Napoleon's Marshalls), his statue is in the town square. But who is the other? Could be a question for later!

Still passing numerous war graves cemeteries as I head towards Mons where the British Expeditionary Force (BEF) under Sir John French met the oncoming Germans for the first time in 1914.

On now through the valley of the Sambre to Mauberge for lunch. Pass first friterie outside Mauberge – a sign of things to come I suspect as I approach Belgium. Also I have first altercation with French driver. Mercedes (say no more) decides he wants to push me in the gutter. I hold my ground and receive loud blast from car horn. As it sweeps past I shake my fist. Then 400 yards down the road, it has had to stop for traffic lights. I pull nonchalantly along side and look in the window. Very pleasant-looking blond lady is scowling at me. I offer a smile but she sweeps off in a huff when the lights turn green. So much for the Entente Cordiale, I guess it's off again. Roll on Belgium, I say.

Stop in Mauberge for proverbial frites and two glasses of beer. Not a very impressive place – very 1960s-looking. Guess it was largely rebuilt after the war. Did enjoy passing remains of Vauban's very impressive fortifications though on my way up to the border via Malplaquet.

Malplaquet was Marlborough's bloodiest victory and an obelisk marks the position defended by Marshal Villars in 1709. Our army, although it contained more Germans than English, lost 25,000 men securing its victory. The field itself, on the northern edge of the Forest of Mormal, is quite small compared with the Somme yesterday.

I cross the border just north of Malplaquet at Blaregnies. No one bothers with my passport so I sweep onto Mons. Very attractive, car-free centre with cobbled streets. There is some entertainment going on in the Grand Place – a music concert and jugglers, I think. Nice of them to lay on such a welcome for me.

Tomorrow, the highlight of the tour pour moi, Waterloo!

Quiz:
1) Who was that other famous son of Le Cateau?
2) What was the nickname given to the soldiers in the BEF in 1914? (I will accept both answers)
3) One of Marlborough's other great victories in Germany in 1704 became the name of the house given to him by the Queen. Tell me what it is called?
4) One of his descendents became a very famous Prime Minister. Who was he?

And as a last bit of fun, let me have your most famous Belgian. Note that Hercules Poirot and Tintin don't count as they are not real!

Off the Road

Lunch: Frites and hamburger in friterie in Mauberge. And a beer or two (it is Saturday!). Hamburger was rubbish but frites marvellous.

Dinner: Pizza parlour in Mons. Slumming it tonight after last few gourmand nights. Plus, Devos, best restaurant in town since 1928, is full! So it's pizza in the Grand Place. Listening to deafening rock music from the concert. Try champignons plus salami pizza. With a carafe of red wine. Actually not too bad.

The Château de Ligny

French Renault tank in Maubeuge

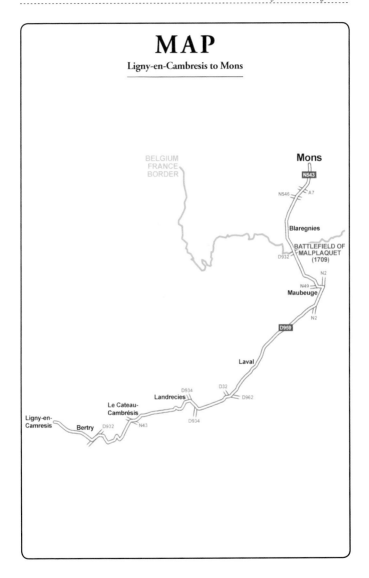

MAP

Ligny-en-Cambresis to Mons

BELGIUM
FRANCE
BORDER

Mons

N543

N546   A7

Blaregnies

**BATTLEFIELD OF
MALPLAQUET
(1709)**

D932

N2

N49

Maubeuge

N2

D959

Laval

D32

D934   D962

Landrecies

Le Cateau-
Cambrésis

Ligny-en-
Camresis   **Bertry**   D932   N43   D934

_Day 14 —————— Mons to Waterloo

Date: 28 May 2006   **42** miles

Waterloo Day! I think, although it's Sunday, that we can have a quiz today. The reason being is that Belgium is part Protestant, I think the Walloons. Albeit I am still in the Catholic bit with the Flemings I do think we can press on. I have to say I am glad I am not a Flem!

Left a quieter Mons (after last night's rock concert) at 8.30am. It is a busy day today – about 40 miles to Waterloo and then the business!

Take N6 north, the main road to Brussels, in order to pass S.H.A.P.E. Stands rather incongruously now and rather amusingly the derelict grounds are now playing host to a Belgian car boot sale! Just down the road is Casteau, where the British army fired its first (August 1914) and last (November 1918) shots of the First World War.

Branched off the main road and met several groups of cyclists en-route to Soussignes where I stopped for coffee. Hardliners these Belgians, very busy bar even at 9.30 in the morning, all middle-aged to late-aged men drinking large glasses of beer! Real men! Put best gruff voice on to order coffee, and then to make it more palatable to the beer drinkers, I make it a strong one and serve it with a Porto. It may be early in the morning but I need fortifying.

Pressed on cross country and across the valley of the Samme to Ittre, Ohain and Braine L'Alleud where a market and that old proverbial Belgian favourite, the rock show, was in full swing! They do seem to like their rock music the Belgians! Sat in the square and had a beer with a barbecued sausage in a baguette. Oh, I forgot to say the sun has decided to put in an appearance today. Not a lot, just a bit. Bless him!

Managed to take wrong road out of Braine L'Alleud after lunch – Sat Nav doesn't seem to work in Belgium. I thought the French road signs were bad but anything other than a motorway doesn't seem to warrant a sign. Anyway, at just before 1.30pm, I see sign for Waterloo and then just after, I spot the Lion Mound itself.

The set up here at Waterloo is quite incredible. A tremendous show. Starts with a sort of audio visual show on the positions of the armies and monuments. Then moves on to a film show with clips from Bondarchuks classic 1970 film to show the main engagements in the battle itself. Then its up the Lion Mount (or Butte de Lion here) to get a fantastic view of the ground. 226 steps to the top which is 41m up. Built over two years and finished in 1826, it serves as a memorial to all the soldiers who died in the battle. Last up is The Panorama, built in 1912, it houses a huge canvas by the French painter Louis Demoulin. It is circular around the wall and covers the battle situation at 4pm on the day. Knock out – that's all I can say.

I hop on my bike to ride round around the battlefield and see Hougoumont (shielded by trees from the Lion Mount) defended superbly by the Grenadier Guards, Plancenoit (where the Prussians arrived late in the day to help Wellington secure the victory), La Belle Alliance (where Wellington met Blucher after the battle was won, incidentally it's now a restaurant and La Haye Sainte (defended stoutly by the Kings German Legion until captured by the French). Up the last ridge to where Wellington viewed the battle and finally the spot where Picton died helping to rebut the advance of the French infantry. Wearing incidentally his civilian frock coat and top hat.

There isn't room here to cover the battle in detail. Suffice it to say it was Napoleon's last throw of the dice had he attempted to split the allied armies and defeat them piecemeal. Wellington, in charge of the British and Belgian army, was having it. Never defeated by Napoleon's generals, he was now up against the man himself. 72,000 French launched themselves all day against 68,000 British, Dutch and Belgians. At the day's end, the Prussians arrived to batter the weakened French and even a final onslaught from Napoleons Old Guard could not save him the day. 42,000 men from both sides lay on the field dead and dying. Prompting Wellington's famous line 'nothing other than a battle lost can be half as melancholy as a battle won'.

Quiz:

1) The names of Napoleon's and Wellington's horses – both of which carried their masters at Waterloo.

2) Who played General Picton in the 1970 film?

3) Who played Marshal Ney?

4) We all know where Napoleon was taken to exile but where did he want to go?

5) What is/was S.H.A.P.E.?

A truly memorable day. And unfortunately the last of my battlefields on this tour. I fear no more vineyards either!

Off the Road

Lunch: Outside bar in Braine L'Alleud. A barbecued Belgian sausage inside a baguette avec two glasses of beer. Sausage surprisingly good.

Dinner: Les Suceries in the Grand Hotel Waterloo. Having a quick pre-cinema dinner tonight as I am going ter pictures love, to see *The Da Vinci Code*. Order Australian fillet steak (by eck that has cum a long way for my tea!) and frites (staple diet here in Belgium but they are good). With a half bottle of Château Pomys 1998 (St Estephe). Wine excellent – a new one on me, a Cru Bourgeois – solid nose and bags of fruit. No length though. Steak cooked perfectly, au point, and chips very good. Served with grilled tomato, braised celery and pepper sauce. I have to say it was much better than I thought it would be.

The Lion Mound at Waterloo

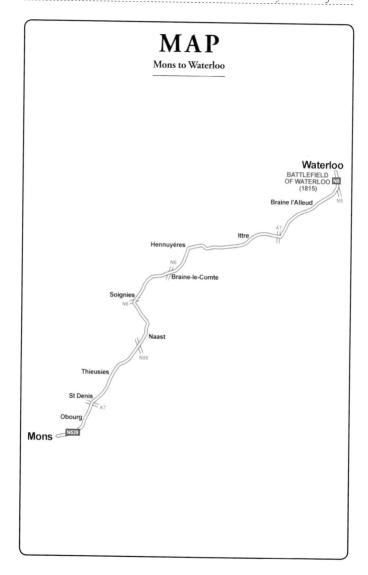

MAP

Mons to Waterloo

_Day **15**———————————— Waterloo to Ghent

Date: 29 May 2006   **60** miles

Two weeks ago to the day that I started this journey of discovery, I left a dark and wet Waterloo for the two day ride to the Channel port of Zeebrugge. Monday morning blues here in Belgium as no Bank Holiday, it seems as everyone goes back to work. Twelve miles through Braine-le-Château and Tubize and I decide it's coffee time. While I do, so the sun pokes through. Hooray!

Get lost finding my way out of Tubize, honestly these Belgians really must do something about their road signs, like try having some! After four miles, find myself on the road to Mons – been there, done that. So I turn around and 15 minutes later I find myself at the coffee shop in Tubize again. Stop the world, I want to get off!

Try again using the navigation technique as my map only has a brown splodge for my current position. Eventually find minor road to Peppingham and from there to Ninove and Aalst for lunch.

After lunch cross the River Scheldt at Wichelen and on into Gent (or Gand in Flemish) for overnight stop in perhaps the most scenic town in Flanders. With medieval buildings, narrow cobbled streets and canals, it needs more time to explore than I have today.

Incidentally, I forgot to report back on everyone's favourite Belgian among all that excitement at Waterloo. Well, I have to go with Mr Chadwick and Eddie Merckx (not sure if that's spelt right), a man after my own heart. Even though Georges Simenon and Rubens (and there's me thinking he was Dutch!) were mentioned in dispatches.

I should bring you my up to date on my mileages. I have now completed 1,015 miles and by my reckoning have now got about 120 to go to Burley-in-Wharfedale. Which will certainly mean I will eclipse the 1,097 miles I did between Lands End and John O'Groats two years ago. Last leg to the Channel tomorrow.

Quiz: Gent is in Flanders, part of Belgium since it was given its independence in 1830 but which two former European Super Powers used to own and govern Flanders and which Royal family of Europe links them?

Off the Road

Lunch: Croque Monsieur and a coke in bar on the edge of the Grand Place in Aalst. A beautiful Flemish town with very grand church with clock tower. Munch on a few of my left over nuts from Braine L'Alleud yesterday. Sun is peeking out once more after torrential downpour in Ninove.

Dinner: Peking Victoria in Gent. Chinese at last! In, supposedly, the oldest chinese restaurant in Gent. I'm dying for some Chinese scran after all that gourmet cooking. Not a good sign when I get a knife and fork instead of chopsticks though. What have I done? Chinese spicy king prawns. Four large king prawns served 'butterfly' style on a bed of lettuce with orange?? Slices. Covered with 'hot' sauce. Messy – prawns quite tasty but not hot at all! Sauce more garlic than spicy. Bit of a disappointment that. Beef fillet Cantonese-style with black bean sauce served with yoeung chow fried rice. Nice enough beef but it's all a bit so so. I think I'm ready for home now and the little lady's spag bol, chilli and greek chicken. Bring it on! All washed down with a half bottle of Sancerre.

The main square in Aalst, Belgium

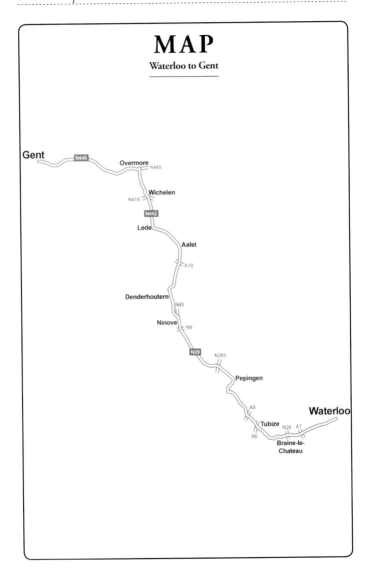

MAP

Waterloo to Gent

_Day 16

Gent to Zeebrugge

Date: 30 May 2006

43 miles

It's a sunny start to the day here in Gent. And the forecast for Hull and the north of England looks good for tomorrow. Bloomin' typical – I travel over 1,000 miles from the south west of France in probably the worst weather for many years and just as I get home it decides to warm up! Still perhaps the sun will help with Rooney's foot!

Leave Gent to the north west in a 21mph north westerly! Arrive after 12 miles in Kaprijke and look for coffee shop. Then find out that most of Belgium is shut on a Tuesday! Eventually, find a 'broot' shop and nice lady makes me a ham sandwich, but no coffee.

Some very good bike paths here in Belgium, only problem is quality of surface, usually lots of gravel and debris that's blown over from the road. Hence, need to watch closely, I don't want another puncture now. Cross the Leopold Canal outside St Laureins and find myself in Holland! Not expecting to visit another country this trip! Then the unthinkable, it starts to hail. Viscious little hail stones pound my face so I cross back into Belgium at Eede. Must be a sign – this trip is supposed to be Catholic countries only!

About an hour later I reach Heist, not today, so turn left into Zeebrugge.

Arrive breathless and just before the next rain shower in Zeebrugge at 1.15pm. Decide to have a big lunch before getting on the ferry. Unfortunately, De Barcadere's restaurant is closed, permanently! Disaster, Zeebrugges's two Michelin-starred restaurants are closed on Tuesdays. Then as if by divine intervention, and just as I was about to join the queue outside the friterie, I espied 'New Corner' at the side of what appears to be a new building development. Glanced through the window to see welcoming sight of oyster bar. In seconds, I am seated comfortably by a window with a view of the building development and rain squalls. Now, where's that ferry, I need to lay down?

Wind almost impossible to ride against and struggle last two miles to the ferry terminal but see The Pride of York and heart lifts and gets me over the line. 40 miles cycled today, the lowest of the tour, and lowest average of 10.1mph. Nice lady at check-in allocates me a deluxe cabin, which seems to mean I get a voucher for tomorrow morning's greasy breakfast. Bring back the bits of baguette I say!

Well the tour is nearly over and, although I will reflect more fully tomorrow as I wing my way through Yorkshire, I think it is appropriate to thank France for her food and wine of which, as you know, I have partaken fully these last two weeks. Back to egg and chips for me, that is, of course, if Lizzie allows! I can report now that I lost over a stone and two inches on my waist through the cycling but unfortunately put on a stone and gained 2 inches dining a la gourmet!

Quiz: As I start my short voyage back to Yorkshire, it reminds me of that classic 1958 film, *A Night to Remember*.
1) What was the ship?
2) Who played the hero? Back in touch in the morning... I hope!

Off the Road

Lunch: A great find – an oyster bar in Zeebrugge. The oysters and Sancerre are excellent so I proceeded to the cod and lobster main course. Finish with apple pie and ice cream. What a find! It was a wonderful meal, with good wine.

The old cobbled streets in Gent

The castle in Gent

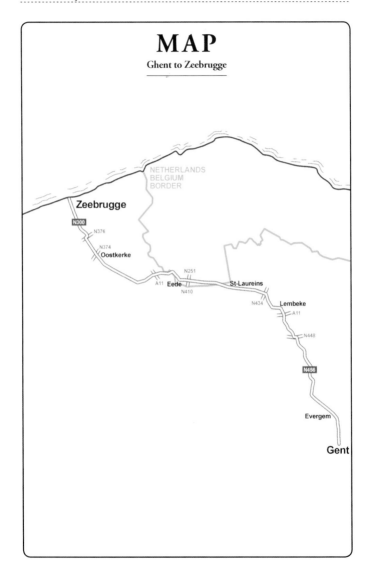

MAP

Ghent to Zeebrugge

_Day 17 ———— Hull to Burley-in-Wharfedale

Date: 31 May 2006   **78** miles

Wake up in the King George V dock in Hull. Blighty at last! One greasy breakfast later and I hit the road at 8am. Queue at customs, so nip around the outside and pedal like hell. Don't want pulling now, what with all these Belgian chocolates in my panniers!

Follow dismal road through Hull and look for coffee stop in Hessle, nope, North Ferriby, nope, Elloughton, nope, South Cave, nope, until at last I find one in Howden. They've run out of teacakes so I settle for toast and a custard tart with my coffee.

As I cycle through God's own county, with the sun shining down out of a blue sky I can reflect on the last two and a bit weeks. My 'top five' results appear at the back of the book. For now, the hits and misses, well a big, big hit was the food. The biggest 'miss'. Well it has to be the weather in France. My suntan cream is hardly used and my brown pigment is due to rust rather than sun! I didn't see the sun for 11 days running and it rained most days. Can you believe it?

After lunch in a nice pub, join the River Wharfe just south of Tadcaster. Not literally I might add. I can follow it all the way home. Glorious Wharfedale! As I pedal back home my thoughts also turn to ideas for the 2008 tour. One possibility is for an Iberian Tour, following Wellington's route from Lisbon and the lines of the Torres Vedras to Toulouse as he chased the French out of Spain. Some great battlefields, beautiful food and excellent wine. Let me know what you think and of any suggestions you can give me for the 2008 tour.

Finally, after 78 miles today, I arrive in Burley-in-Wharfedale to a heroes welcome. Actually, Lizzie was sweeping the drive and asked me not to make a mess! Que sera, sera!

⬛⬛⬛ *Off the Road*

Lunch: Find a nice pub – the Castle Inn in Cawood on the River Ouse for lunch. Scampi and chips, great British food Plus a pint of John Smiths.

My final statistics for the trip are:
1,136 miles
At an average speed of 11.4 mph
Maximum speed 39.8 (between Alençon and Douains on Day 8)

Au revoir mes amies.

The Castle Inn at Cawood

The hero returns to Burley and a freshly swept drive!

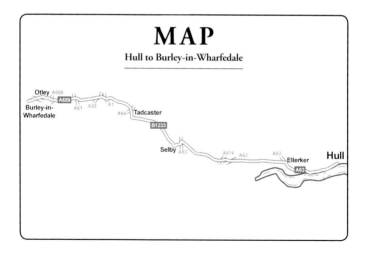

Bordeaux to Burley-in-Wharfedale

Bike Ride

15 May to 31 May 2006

The Route

Key:
L = Left
R = Right
S.P. Sign posted
Distance Miles

DAY 1 – Monday 15 May: St Quentin de Baron to Royan

0   Minor Roads to D120. D120 to D239. Turn R to

3   **Le Sauve** Pick up Bike Path towards **Bordeaux** passing:- **Creon, Sadirac, Lignan de B, L'Atresne** and

17   **Pont Francois Mitterand**. Stay on right bank (D113) to **Pont de Pierre** to cross the River Garonne. Stay on Left Bank road to **Bacalan** and under Pont d'Aquitaine to D209. Follow D209 towards **Blanquefort**. Take next R on D209 to

30   **St Louis de Montferand** Continue on D209 to

34   **Macau** Continue NW and join D2 at. **Siran**. D2 to

40   **Margaux** **Lunch** Continue on D2 to **Cussac Beycheville** and

50.5   **St Julien** continue on D2 to R Turn on D2 E4 after **Pichon Longueville**. Follow road on River Bank to

53   **Pauillac** Continue by River Bank (D2 E4) to

58   **St Estephe** Stay by River Bank to

60   **St Sevrin de Cadourne** Take D2 to **Port de la Marechale** and

63.5   **St Yzans de Medoc**

66   **St Christoly-Medoc**

71   **Valeyrac**

79   Outskirts of **St Vivien de Medoc**. Take D1E4 N to

81.5   **Talais** and **Neyran**. Turn R to join N215 to **Le Verdon sur Mer** and

90.5   **Pointe de Grave Ferry** Take ferry to Royan. From Harbour follow road to Palais des Congress then onto Avenue de Pontaillac. Hotel is on the Right after approx 1 mile.

DAY 2 – Tuesday 16 May: Royan to Ile de Re

0   Follow coast road out of **Royan** to **Pontaillac**, **Nauzan** and

4   **St Palais** – Follow coast road to **La Grande Cote** and Turn L on D25 to

10   **La Palmyre** Turn R on D141E to

11	**Les Mathes** Continue on D141 to
12.5	**Arvert** Bear L on old D14 thru **Le Maine Geay** to
14	**La Tremblade Cont** on towards **Ronce les Bains** but turn on D728 to
21	**Marennes** – visit Oyster Museum at **Bourcefranc le Chapus**. Leave **Marennes** on D3 to
25.5	**Brouage** Cont on D3 over salt marshes to
31.5	**Soubise** Cross over La Charente and cont into **Rochefort** or Turn R on D238 to D733. Turn L to cross the River Charente into
37	**Rochefort** Lunch. Take D5 N to **Breuil-Magne** After 5 miles Turn L on D111 to
48	**Ballon** Cont on D111 through **Thaire** onto D203 to **St Vivien**. Turn L on D113 to
56	**Chatelaillon Plage** Turn R on D202 to **St Jean des Sables Angoulins Aytre**
64.5	**La Rochelle**. Head for Harbour and then Cathedral St Louis (Rue de Palais and Rue Chaudrier) Turn L on D21 (Av Gen Leclerc) to the
71	Bridge for Isle de Re. Take D735 to
76	**La Flotte Cont** to re-join D735 and onto
78	**St Martin de Re**

DAY 3 – Wednesday 17 May: Isle de Re to Melle

0	Follow D735 back to the
6	Pont Viaduc Turn L on D106 to
10	**L'Houmeau** Turn R on D104 to
12.5	**Lagord** Take D105 N to a R Turn to
14	**Puilboreau** Take 106 N towards **St Xandre** Turn R on D107 to
17	**Dompierre** Keep on D107 to
20	**Bourgneuf** Take D203 S to
22.5	**Clavette** Turn L in village on D108 to
30	**Virson** Keep on D108 to
34.5	**Vouhe** Turn R on D115 S to
39	**Surgeres**. Lunch. Take D111 to
47.5	**Marsais** stay on D111 to L Turn to D53 to
55	**Prisse la Charriere** Stay on D53 through the **Foret de Chize** to
59.5	**Virolfet** Cross over D1 onto D119 to **Vaubalier** and
68	**Perigne** Take D103 and then first R on D101 E to **Mezieres**, **St Romans les Melle** and
75	**Melle**

DAY 4 – Thursday 18 May: Melle to St Benoit (Poitiers)

0	Leave **Melle** on D14 and D950 (NE towards **Poitiers**). After 1 mile turn R on D14 to
8	**Lezay** Continue on D14 to
20	**Couhe** Leave **Couhe** on D2 NE to
26	**Anche** Cont on D2 to
34.5	**Gencay** LUNCH? Go thru **St Maurice-la-Clouere** and onto D1 N to
40	**Gizay** Cont on D1 to
44	**Nieuil-l'Espoir** Turn L on D12 NW to
47	Nouaille-Maupertuis Monuments to Battle of Poitiers 1356. Leave **Maupertuis** on D12 N. After 1.5 miles Turn L on D12c towards **Poitiers**. After 0.5 miles Turn L to **Flee** Cont to D741 Turn R to
53.5	**St Benoit**

DAY 5 – Friday 19 May: St Benoit to Fontevraud l'Abbaye

0	Take D741 N to
3	**Poitiers**. Go thru centre of town to the River Clain and take D4 N to
7	**Bonnillet** Keep on D4 to
10	St Georges les Baillargeaux Cont on D4 to
13	**Dissay** and
14.5	**St Cyr** and **La Varenne** Turn L to
18	La Moussais la Bataille. Battle of Tours 732 Cont on to **Domine** and cross the River Clain to
20	**Naintre** Take the D23 N to
25.5	**Scorbe-Clairvaux** Take the D725 W to
30	**Lencloitre** Take the D20 NW to
34	**Doussay** Take the D68 to
42	**Monts-s-Guesnes** Lunch? Take D14 N to
47	**La Roche-Rigault** cont on D14 to
52.5	**Loudun** Take the D147 N to
61.5	**Roiffe** cont on D147 N to
66.5	**Fontevraud l'Abbaye**

DAY 6 – Saturday 20 May: Fontevraud l'Abbaye to Loué

0	Go N to re-join D947 to
3	**Montsoreau** Turn L on D947 to
11	**Saumur** Go thru the town staying on the Left Bank of the River Loire.

heading for **St Florent** and **St Hilaire** Take D751 to

21.5	**Gennes** Turn R over the River Loire on D751 to **Les Rosiers sur Loire**. Take D59 N to
29	**Beaufort en Vallee** Leave village on N147 W to
33.5	**Maze** Turn R off the main road and pick up D74 to
37.5	**Baune** Stay on D74 and cross over A85 and A11 to
44.5	**Seiches sur le Loir** Lunch? Cross the River Loir on D74 to
48	**Montreuil s Loir** 0.5m after village Turn R on D89 to
52	**Etriche** Take D52 N to
59	**Morannes** Stay on D52 for 2 miles then Turn L on D18 to
64	**Precigne** Leave village N on D24 to
70.5	**Sable sur Sarthe** Cross River Sarthe and Turn R on D4 to
77	**Poille sur Vegre** Cont to
81	**Brulon** Turn R on D21 to
85	**Loué**

DAY 7 – Sunday 21 May: Loué to Alencon

0	Leave **Loué** on D101 N. Cross over A81 and Turn L on D93 to
5	**Chemire en Charnie** Turn R on D4 to
10	**Parennes** Cont on D4 to
17	**Sille-le-Guillaume** Lunch? Take D310 NE to
26.5	**Freshay s. Sarthe**. Take D15 N to
29.5	**Asse le Boisne** Take D21 N to
32.5	**Guesnes le Gandelin** Take D30 N to
38.5	**Alencon**. Follow road thru **Alencon** past Notre Dame Cathedral on the Right. Hotel is on the L.

DAY 8 – Monday 22 May: Alencon to Douains

0	Take D112 and then D31 NE out of **Alencon** to
6.5	**Menil - Evreux** Continue on D31 to
10	**Essay** Stay on D31 Then L on D4 to
18.5	**Courtomer** Take D3 in village to
24.5	**Moulins-la-Marche** Stay on D3 to **Auguaise** and then cross N26 to
35	**L'Aigle** Lunch Take D930 NE to
40.5	**Rugles le Moulin** Take D141 E to
50	**Breteuil-sur-Iton** Take D833 E to
58.5	**Damville** Cont on D833 and then L on D51 N to **Garel** cont and cross N2134 to

67.5	**Angerville-la-Campagne** (just S of **Evreux**) Cont to cross N154 to
70.5	**Le Coudray** Turn R on lane to **St Aubin** Cont on D67 to
72.5	**Le Vieil-Evreux** Cont to **Cierrey** and
75.5	**Caillouet** Cross N13 to **St Aquilin-de-Pacy** Cont to D71. Turn L to
78	**Croisy sur Eure** Turn R on D65 to cross the River Eure to **Menilles** and on to cross D181 on D533 to
82	**Douains**

DAY 9 – Tuesday 23 May: Douains to Aumale

0	Take D75 N to **Brecourt** Turn R on D181 to
6	**Vernon** Cross the River Seine and turn R on D5 to **Giverny** and
12	**Gashy** Stay on D5 to **Fourges** and
16.5	**Bray-et-Lu** Take a Left on D146 to **St Remy**, **Aveny** and
21	**Bordeaux-St-Clair** Stay on D146 to
25	**Dangu** Turn R on D981 and L on D915 to
29	**Gisors** Lunch? Take D14 N to
31.5	**Bazincourt-sur-Epte** Stay on D914 to **Thierceville** Cross the River Epte to
34	**Serifontaine** Take D914 N to **Talmontiers**, **Bouchevilliers** and
39	**Neuf-Marche** Continue on D915 to
43	**Gournay-en-Bray** Take D916 N to
48.5	**Bazancourt** Take D316 N to
51.5	**Samson-la-Poterie** Cont on D316 to **Courcelles Campeaux** and Turn L on D150 to
55	**Boutavent** Stay on D150 to R turn on D316 to
57	**Blargies** Stay on D316 to **Abancourt** After 1 mile Turn R on D69 to
61	**Gourchelles** Turn L on D68 to **Quincampoix** and **Fleuzy** Turn R on D316 to
64	**Aumale**

DAY 10 – Wednesday 24 May: Aumale to Montreuil

0	Take D49 N to
3	**Guemicourt** Continue to
5	**Rouen-sur-Bresle** Continue to
7	**Hodeng sur Bresle** Continue to
8	**Senarpont** Continue to
12.5	**Blangy sur Bresle** Cross River Bresle and head N on D928 to
16	**Le Transley** stay on D928 to

19	**St Maxent** stay on D928 to
27.5	**Abbeville** Lunch Leave **Abbeville** NNE on unmarked lane to
31	**Drucat** Take L turn to Le Plessiel cross D928 and continue to **Ouville** and
34	**Hautvillers** Take R turn on D105 to **Lamotte Buleux** and
36	**Forest L'Abbaye** Stay on D105 and then D111 to
40	**Crecy en Ponthieu** Battle of Crecy Monuments – **Crecy**, Monument on D56 towards **Fontaine**, Moulin Edward III, **Estrees**, **Wadicourt**. Head N on D111 to
47	**Dompierre sur Authie** Cross River Authie and Turn L on D119 to
50	**Douriez** Stay on D119 to
54	**Maintenay** and
55.5	**Roussent** Turn R on D139 N to
58	**Boisjean** Stay on D119 to
62	**Montreuil**

DAY 11 – Thursday 25 May: Montreuil to Arras

0	**Leave Montreuil** on D349 SE to
6	**Lespinoy** Continue on D349 to
10	**Aubin St Vaast** Turn L and cross River Canche on D154 to
13.5	**Cauron St Martin** Stay on D154 to
17	**Planques** Turn R on D107 to cross D928 to
18.5	**Bucamps** Turn L to
20	Agincourt Battle of Agincourt monuments at **Tramecourt** and **Mainsoncelle**. Take D104 to
25.5	**Blangy sur Ternoise** Stay on D104 to **Humerueville** and thru village to R Turn on D39 then L on D41 to
32.5	**St.Pol sur Ternoise** Lunch Take D916 S to **Herlin le Sec** and then L Turn on D23 to
36	**Buneville**. Stay on D23 to
38.5	**Houvin-Houvigneul** Cont on D23 to
40.5	**Estree-Wamin** Turn L on Gr121 to **Berlencourt** and R Turn on D79 to
43.5	**Liencourt** Turn L on D339 to
46.5	**Avesnes le Comte** Take D68 to
50	**Wanquetin** Take D59 to
52.5	**Warlus**
55	**Dainville**
57	**Arras**

DAY 12 – Friday 26 May: Arras to Ligny-en-Cambresis

0	Leave **Arras** S on D919 to
6.5	**Boiry St Martin** Turn R on D35 to
8.5	**Adinfer** Stay on D35 to
12.5	**Hennescamps** Head S on D3 to
14	**Foncquevillers** . Somme Battlefield. Take D6 to **Gommecourt** Turn R to
16	**Hebuterne** Go S on D28 and D174 to the D4129. Turn L to cross D919 to the D163. Take a L Turn to
20	**Beaumont Hamel** Take D4151 to the D50. Turn R to cross the River Ancre at
24	**Authuile**. Turn L on the D151 to
24.5	**Thiepval** Turn R on D73 to to
26.5	**Pozieres** Turn L on D929 and immediately R on D73 to
28	**Bazentin** Turn R on D107 to
30.5	**Longueval** Go L on D197 to **Flers** and R Turn to
33.5	**Ginchy** Go S to a L Turn on D20 to
35.5	**Combles** Lunch Take D172 under the A1 to
38.5	**Sailly-Saillisel** continue on D172 to
40.5	**Mesnil-en-Arrouaise** Cont on D172 to the D58. Take D58 to
45.5	**Fins** Turn L on D55. Then D17 to
47.5	**Metz en Couture** Take D17 to
50	**Trescault** Take D29 to
52	**Ribecourt la Tour** Cont on D29 over the A26 to
54	**Marcoing** Cross the Canal to the D15 to
56.5	**Rumilly-en-Cambresis**. Cambrai Battlefield. Take the D142 to **Crevecoeur** and then the D15 to
60	**Lesdain** Cont on D15 to
61.5	**Esnes** Cont on D15 to
62.5	**Haucourt en Cambresis** cont on D15 to
64	**Ligny en Cambresis**

DAY 13 – Saturday 27 May: Ligny-en-Cambresis to Mons

0	Take D16 N out of **Ligny** towards **Caudry** but Turn R to
1.5	**Montigny-en-Cambresis** Continue to the D98 and take a L turn to
3.5	**Bertry** Take D115 to
5	**Maurois** Take a L turn on the D932 to
5.5	**Reumont** Take a R Turn to the D21. Turn L on D21 and then R to
8.5	**St Benin** Take the D67 L (N) to

11	**Le Cateau**. Take N43 SE to a L Turn on the D959 to
13	**Pommereuil** Cont on the D959 to
18	**Landrecies** Cont on the D959 to
21.5	**Maroilles** Cont on D959 to
26.5	**Laval** Cont on the D959 to
29	**Bachant** Cont on D959 to
31.5	**St Remy** Cont on D959 to
34.5	**Hautmont** Take the N2 into
36	**Maubeuge** Lunch Head for the Church of St Pierre St Paul on Avenue. Franklin Roosevelt. Cont to the roundabout and take the 1st exit (Avenue Porte-de-Bavay). Cont to the D105 to
39	**Fort de Leveue** Cont to a R Turn on the D159 N. After 0.5 miles Turn L to cross border into Belgium to
42.5	**Blaregnies** Leave N on N543 to
45.5	**Norchain** Cont into
49	**Mons**

DAY 14 – Sunday 28 May: Mons to Waterloo

0	Leave **Mons** NE on N539 to
3.5	**Obourg** Continue N under A7 to
5	**St Denis**. Cont N to
7	**Thieusies** Cont N to
8	**Sirieux** Cont NE to cross N55 to
10.5	**Naast** Turn L NW to
13	**Soignes** Continue on backroads to
16.5	**Braine le Comte** Continue on lanes NE to
19	**Hennuyeres** and
20	**Ardennes** Turn E to
23.5	**Ittre** Continue under the A7 to
26	**Bois** Go NE to
28	**Ophain** and
30	**Braine l'Alleud** Lunch Go E to
31	**Butte de Lion** Start the circular tour of the Waterloo Battlefield. Go N on the N5 to
40.5	**Waterloo**

DAY 15 – Monday 29 May: Waterloo to Ghent

0	Leave **Waterloo** W on unmarked road to **Mont St Pont** Continue to go

	under A7/E19 to
6	**Braine-le-Chateau** Continue on to **Niderand** and
9.5	**Tubize** Continue NW to go over A8 to the N7. Turn R then immediately L to
13	**Bogaarden** Turn R to **Bellingen** and L at the N28 to
15	**Pepingen** Continue on the N28 to
17	**Leerbeck** Continue on N28 to **Meerbeke** and L at N8 into
23.5	**Ninove** Head N on unmarked road parallel to N45 to
26	**Denderhoutern** Cont thru **Daal** and on to a R Turn on the N460 under the N45 and into
31	**Aalst** Lunch Leave N on Katte Street to cross the R41 and cont N on unmarked road to L Turn to
34	**Lede** Head N on N442 to
37	**Wichelen** Cont N thru **Uitbergen** to
40	**Overmere** Go L on N445 thru **Kruisen** to
46.5	**Destelbergen** Continue into
50	**Gent**

DAY 16 – Tuesday 30 May: Ghent to Zeebrugge

0	Leave **Ghent** N on N458 and N456 to
4.5	**Evergem** Continue on N456 to
6	**Sleidinge** Cont on N456 to
8.5	**Vierhuizen** Cont on N456 to
11	**Lembeke** Cont on N456 to
12.5	**Kaprijke** Turn L on unmarked roads to
14	**D'Hoogte** Cross N434 to **Het Kruisen** and
17	**St-Laureins** Lunch Cont on unmarked roads to **Moershoofde** and **Vuilpan** and
20.5	**Eede** Cont on unmarked roads to
22	**Middelburg** Continue to Leopold Canal. Follow Canal on N bank to **Molentje Platheule**
28.5	**Oostkerke** Cont on to **Eienbroek** Turn R on unmarked road to a L Turn on N376 and then R on N300 to
32	**Ramskapelle** Continue into **Heist** and L into
36.5	**Zeebrugge** Head for Car Ferry Terminal (P&O). Ferry to Hull leaves at 19.00 hours

DAY 17 – Wednesday 31 May: Hull to Burley

0	Leave Ferry Terminal on A1033 L into
2.5	**Hull** Take A63 and minor roads out of **Hull** to the
8	Humber Bridge Take minor roads to
10.5	North Ferriby Take minor roads to
12.5	**Welton** Minor roads to
14	**Elloughton** Minor Roads to
16	**Ellerker** Minor roads to
17.5	North Cave Take a L Turn on B1230 to
21.5	**Gilberdyke** Cont on B1230 to
26.5	**Howden** At Church take a R Turn on A63 (sp Selby) to **Hemingbrough** Cont on A63 to
34.5	**Barlby** Turn L into
36	**Selby** Lunch R Turn on B1233 to
40	**Cawood** Cont on B1233 to **Ryther**
46	**Ulleskelf** Cont on B1233 to the A162. Turn R to
47.5	**Tadcaster** Go R on A659 and then immediately L on A659 to
52	**Boston Spa** Cont on A659 to
54	**Collingham** Cont on A659 to
57.5	**Harewood**
62.5	**Pool**
64.5	**Otley**
68	**Burley-in-Wharfedale**

Daily Quiz Answers

DAY 2
James Bond (most went for Sean Connery but I wanted the character's name).
Sylvia Trench (in the Ambassadors Club in London at the start of *Doctor No*)
– Bond went on to romance the delectable Miss Trench at the start of *From Russia with Love*. He had Champagne in the glove box of his Bentley. A nice trick if you can afford it! The Bentley that is!

DAY 3
Silver. Charlemagne, the first Holy Roman Emperor, used it for making his coins.

DAY 4
Edward III and **good longbowmen**.

DAY 5
1) **Herbert Lom** 2) **Granada**, and the trick question, Charles Martel had **absolutely nothing** to do with the Cognac bearing his name.

Day 6: **Warwick, mushrooms, Steve McQueen** and **Poussins**.

Day 8: **Orson Welles, Napoleon.**

Day 9: **Castle Donington.**

Day 10: Charles motto as Prince of Wales is **Ich Dien (I serve)**, taken from the ostrich plumes tied with gold braid on King John of Bohemia's helmet. Originally awarded to the Black Prince and forever handed down to all Prince of Wales since. Charles has it engraved on his tie pin and cufflinks. **Montreuil** was Lord Haig's HQ during the First World War (Haig was overall commander of the British Army in France).

Day 11: **Laurence Olivier.** The film quotes were from: *Marathon Man, Wuthering Heights, Spartacus.* The bonus question was **Anthony Hopkins**.

Day 12: **Kirk Douglas, Stanley Kubrick, Paths of Glory, James Mason, The Blue Max, Little Willie.**

Day 13: **Matisse, Old Contemptibles or Old Bills, Blenheim, Churchill.**

Day 14: Copenhagen (Wellington) and **Marengo** (Napoleon), **Jack Hawkins as General Picton** and **Dan O'Herlihy as Marshal Ney**. **America** is where Napoleon wanted to go. **Supreme Headquarters Allied Powers Europe** – now a car boot sale showground every other Sunday!

Day 15: Spain and Austria. Connected through the Hapsburg family

Day 16: I survived the Titanic and it was Kenneth More playing the hero as the ship went down. Fortunately, my ship, the Pride of York, survived the crossing from Belgium.

Mileages

Bordeaux to Burley-in-Wharfedale by Bike – The Battlefields and Wine Tour

Average Daily Mileage – 62.1

Date	From	To	Miles (Cum)	Av.Speed
May 15	St Quentin de Baron	Royan	95	11.8mph
16	Royan	Isle de Re	78 (173)	11.2mph
17	Isle de Re	Melle	73 (246)	11.1mph
18	Melle	Poitiers	57 (303)	11.7mph
19	Poitiers	Fontevraud l'Abbaye	69.5 (372.5)	10.9mph
20	Fontevraud l'Abbaye	Loue	84.5 (457)	11.4mph
21	Loue	Alencon	40 (497)	12mph
22	Alencon	Douains	90.5 (587.5)	13.2mph
23	Douains	Aumale	71 (658.5)	12.2mph
24	Aumale	Montreuil	70 (728.5)	11.1mph
25	Montreuil	Arras	66 (794.5)	11.7mph
26	Arras	Ligny-en-Cambresis	64 (858.5)	11.6mph
27	Ligny-en-Cambresis	Mons	54.5 (913)	12.1mph
28	Mons	Waterloo	42 (955)	10.2mph
29	Waterloo	Ghent	60 (1015)	10.7mph
30	Ghent	Zeebrugge	43 (1058)	10.2mph
31	Hull	Burley-in-Wharfedale	78 (1136)	11.6mph

The Battlefields Tour

May 18
The Battle of Poitiers
1356

May 19
The Battle of Tours 732

May 24
The Battle of Crecy 1346

May 25
The Battle of Agincourt
1415

May 26
The Battle of the Somme
1916

May 27
The Battle of Mons 1914

May 28
The Battle of Waterloo
1815

List of stuff I took

CLOTHES

1 pair of shorts
1 pair of trousers
2 pairs of pants
2 pairs of socks
1 shirt
1 t-shirt
1 pair of shoes
1 brown belt
1 pair of swimming
trunks

BIKE CLOTHES

2 pairs of cycling shorts
2 cycling shirts
1 long-sleeved shirt
Wind jacket (yellow)
Rain mac
2 pairs of gloves
Sunglasses
Helmet
Lock
2 pairs of socks
1 base layer
Waterproof shoe covers
Rain pants
Cycling shoes
2 drinking bottles

MISCELLANEOUS

Maps
Wallet – cash/credit cards
Camera and charger
French/English dictionary
PDA and charger
GPS and charger
Memory cards
Notebook and pen
First aid kit
Wash bag and flannel
Travel towel
Plastic bags
Accommodation list
Route instructions
2 paperbacks for reading
2 pegs
Telephone numbers
Bike insurance details
Michelin Guides for
France and Belgium
Battlefields notes
Plastic plate, glass, cutlery

TOOLS

Pump
Puncture repair kit
4 spare inner tubes
Tyre levers
Allen keys
Tool kit/devil
Pliers
Lube
Adhesive tape (insulating)
Zip ties
Small rag
Pressure gauge

MEDICINES

Gaviscon
Paracetamol
Sudacrem
Shorts cream
Sun cream
Lip block
Midge/insect repellent
Ibuleve gel
Plasters
Ibuprofen
Leg toner cream

Accommodation

Date	Accommodation	Telephone
May 15	Grand Hotel de Pontaillac, Royan ①	05 46390044
16	La Jetee Hotel, Ile de Re ②	05 46093636
17	Les Glycines, Melle	05 49270111
18	Chalet de Venise, St Benoit, Poitiers - now closed	05 49884507
19	La Croix Blanche, Fontevraud l'Abbaye ③	02 41517111
20	Hotel Ricordeau, Loue ④	02 43884003
21	Le Grand Cerf, Alençon	02 33260051
22	Château de Brecourt, Douains ⑤	02 32524050
23	Villa des Houx, Aumale ⑥	02 35939330
24	Château de Montreuil, Montreuil ⑦	03 21815304
25	L'Univers, Arras	03 21713401
26	Château de Ligny, Ligny-en-Cambrésis ⑧	03 27852584
27	Infotel, Mons	065 401830
28	The Grand Hotel, Waterloo ⑨	02 3521815
29	The Novotel Centrum, Ghent	09 2242230
30	Car Ferry to Hull ⑩	
31	HOME!	

Verdon – Royan ferry
Tel: 05 56733773
Operates at 15.10, 16.40, 18.25, 19.55

Top five lists

Worst hills

1) A '1in 5' climb north out of the valley of the River Eure from Menille.

2) The climb out of the valley of the River Bresle to Oisemont on the D25.

3) Eastwards up the Pont Viaduc on the D 735 against the wind!

4) Climb away from River Planquette on the D154 near Agincourt.

5) Climb up the D948 into Melle.

Lunch stops

1) The Pavillon de Margaux off the D2 in Margaux – one of my favourite places anywhere in the world!

2) Le Vieux Château below the castle at Gencay (just off the D741).

3) Steak and frites at Restaurant de Poste in St Pol sur Ternaise (off N41)

4) Barbecued sausage sandwich outside the Bar in Brain L'Alleud.

5) Croque Monsieur in a café on the edge of the Grand Place in Aalst.

Overnight stops

1) Château de Montreuil, Montreuil (03 21815304) A Michelin-starred restaurant with great wine and top service. And a very comfy bed!

2) Hotel Ricordeau, Loué (02 43884003) A totally unexpected delight.

3) The Croix de Blanche, Fontevraud (02 41517111). A lovely spot by the Abbey and they washed cycling kit too!

4) Château de Brecourt at Douains (02 32524050). Magnificent 17th-Century château. Great service, but I was only guest!

5) Château de Ligny-en-Cambresis, Ligny

(03 27852584). A modernised château complete with moat and top class restaurant.

Best food lists

* Indicates the best of in each category.

Best starters

Baby asparagus at Les Glycines, Melle.

Langoustines at the Hotel Ricordeau, Loué.*

Breton lobster at the Château de Brecourt.

Ravioli de Homard at Villa des Houx, Aumale.

Asparagus with Parma ham and shitake mushrooms at the Château de Montreuil.

Warm oysters with asparagus and leeks at the Château de Ligny.

Best main courses

Lobster at the Baleine Bleue, Saint-Martin de Re.

Lobster and sole at the Hotel Ricordeau, Loué. *

Sole with squid ink, girolles and baby carrots at the Château de Brecourt.

Fillet de boeuf with fois gras at the Château de Montreuil.

Pigeon at the Chateau de Ligny.

Best pudding
Soufle of molten Chocolate with vanilla ice cream at Les Glycines, Melle.

The cheeses at Hotel Ricordeau, Loue.

Pina colada and peppermint chocolate at Hotel Ricordeau, Loué.

Crepes Suzette at Villa des Houx, Aumale.

Fresh cherries with vanilla emulsion and chocolate sauce at the Château de Montreuil.*

Best Wines
Trimbach Riesling 2000 at the Baleine Blueu, Saint-Martin de Re

Bourgueil 2000 at Hotel Ricordeau, Loué.

St Estephe 1998 at the Château de Brecourt.

Château Haut de Marbouzet 2000 at Château de Montreuil.*

Château Tour de Pez 2001 at Le Clusius, Arras.

Best delightful stops along the way

1) The harbour at Saint-Martin de Re.

2) The fortified town of Brouage near Rochefort (if only I could find the way out!).

3) The market town of Breteuil in southern Normandy.

4) The medieval city of Ghent in Belgium.

5) Market day in Braine L'Alleud near Waterloo.

6) The château at Dissay, north of Poitiers on the River Chain.

7) Aveny on the River Epte south east of Rouen.

8) The view from my bedroom at Pontaillac near Royan.

Most interesting people met on tour

1) The Hells Angels from Norwich in Alencon (oh what a night!).

2) The receptionist at the Croix la Blanche Hotel in Fontevraud (gorgeous and she washed my cycling kit too!)

3) A fellow cyclist, the French Canadian on the road north out of Pauillac.

4) The Cycling Club of Royan at Surgeres.

5) The surly and aggressive French driver near Maubeuge (although she was a blond!)

I know, I can hear you saying, if these are the most interesting people you met, what a sad person you must be. But that's it for the solo long distance cyclist – two stout legs and a vivid imagination is all you need.

Worst weather

1) The thunderstorm on the D728 into Marennes.

2) The rain on the D751 by the River Loire.

3) The wind (northerlies) on the same day as I head north on the D59 to Beaufort-en-Vallee.

4) 35° temperatures on the D111 heading towards the Foret de Chize (although it was to be the last sun I saw for over a week!).

5) The rain on the road into Alencon.

Best chill out stops for a beer and to watch the girls go by!

1) La Rochelle harbour front at about 5pm.

2) Saumur on the River Loire on market day at about 10.30am.

3) The main square in Arras on a bank holiday at about 5pm – girls in fancy dress too!.

4) The Irish Bar in

Poitiers about 8pm.

5) Anywhere in Ghent at about 3pm!

Final thoughts for those that follow!

There are a number of factors that any self-respecting cyclist needs to take into account when planning a long tour in France.

1) You need decent maps, particularly street maps, for any towns and cities you may travel through (or a Sat Nav system). The ISGN series are good for rural use.

2) Planning your daily stops is very important. There are no pubs and few B&B's in France. Most shops and bars close for long lunch breaks (12 to 4pm) and French restaurants tend to stop serving after 1pm (particularly in rural areas). I recommend stocking up with drinks and bananas every morning!

3) Use the cycling lanes where provided.

Although their surfaces can be poor, French drivers do not take kindly to cyclists on the roads if a cycle path is provided.

4) And finally, stop every afternoon for a glass of Porteau (Port) and a noisette. It keeps your spirits up when you are starting to flag.